KAMILA SHAMSIE

WRITERS AND THEIR WORK

SERIES EDITORS:

*Professor Dinah Birch CBE,
University of Liverpool
Professor Dame Janet Beer,
University of Liverpool*

Writers and Their Work, launched in 1994 in association with the British Council, won immediate acclaim for its publication of brief but rigorous critical examinations of the works of distinguished writers and schools of writing. The series embraces the best of modern literary theory and criticism, and features studies of many popular contemporary writers, as well as the canonical figures of literature and important literary genres.

© Copyright 2025 by Peter Morey

First published in 2025 by
Liverpool University Press
4 Cambridge Street
Liverpool L69 7ZU

on behalf of
Northcote House Publishers Ltd
Mary Tavy
Devon PL19 9PY

Peter Morey has asserted the right to be identified as the author of this book in accordance with the Copyright, Designs and Patents Act 1988. All rights reserved. No part of this book may be reproduced, stored in a retrieval system, or transmitted, in any form or by any means, electronic, mechanical, photocopying, recording, or otherwise, without the prior written permission of the publisher.

British Library Cataloguing-in-Publication Data
A catalogue record for this book is available from the British Library

ISBN 978-1-83624-487-5 (hardback)
ISBN 978-1-83624-488-2 (paperback)

Typeset by Carnegie Book Production, Lancaster

KAMILA SHAMSIE

Peter Morey

Contents

Acknowledgements	vii
Note on Editions and Terms	ix
Biographical Outline	xi
1. Introduction: Transnational Writer of Pakistan	1
2. Early Works: *In the City by the Sea* and *Salt and Saffron*	15
3. Echoes of the Past: *Kartography* and *Broken Verses*	25
4. The Webs of History: *Burnt Shadows* and *A God in Every Stone*	39
5. At Home in the World: *Home Fire* and *Best of Friends*	55
6. Conclusion: Fiction, Form, and Freedom	77
Notes	85
Select Bibliography	99
Index	105

Acknowledgements

Many friends and colleagues have helped this book towards its eventual birth: in truth, too many to name. Key moments of assistance have come from Muneeza Shamsie, who commissioned a short piece on Kamila from me for the *Literary Encyclopedia* and later furnished some biographical details. I found myself consumed by the task, amassing far more material than could be accommodated in the brief entry required of me. From there it was a short step to extending the critical readings I had developed and augmenting them with existing scholarship on the novels and an enhanced sense of the thorny history of Pakistan.

Rehana Ahmed, at various moments, has applied a nudge here and a touch there to my thinking about Shamsie's work. Her critical intelligence – enhanced always by a strong sense of the material and representational disadvantages experienced by British Muslims – inspired me to read more deeply and, I hope, better. My first detailed engagement with Shamsie's novels came when writing my book *Islamophobia and the Novel*. It seems only right to nod in the direction of the various scholars from numerous disciplines who helped shaped my thinking about the literary, cultural, and political context in which Shamsie's works have appeared: times that have been unsettling and even unforgiving for heavily scrutinised Muslim communities. These sources are too numerous to name but each has helped develop my understanding of the issues.

One of the greatest debts I owe is to my students at the University of Birmingham who, year after year, bring fresh eyes to bear on Shamsie's work and who provide stimulating insights that keep me on my toes and make me think and rethink. (A particular debt of gratitude is owed to Kirsty Cooke for tracking down Kamila Shamsie's numerous short stories, which are themselves worthy of greater critical attention than I have been able to give them here.) It is a pleasure always to engage with colleagues such as Claire Chambers, Stephen Morton, Anshuman Mondal, Amy Burge, and Roberta Garrett. In addition to their own exemplary scholarship, they provide support, stimulation and fellow-feeling which is always welcome. I also wish to take this opportunity to thank Christabel Scaife and the team at Liverpool University Press for seeing the book through from commissioning to completion.

Pakistan itself has grown to be my home-from-home. The potted version of its story to be found in these pages does no justice at all to the vibrancy of its culture or the energy of its people. Pakistan has given me more than I am able to return, not least the companionship of Amina Yaqin – much more of an expert on Pakistan than I am. Along with our daughters, Maleeha and Laila, she gives the unconditional support I rely on every day. Since the Pakistani branch of our family have lived through some of the twists and turns traced in Shamsie's work, it seems only right that I should end by thanking them all, but in particular Muhammad Yaqin, whose own intellectual curiosity remains an inspiration, who never gives up, and who always sees the best in people. It is to him that this book is dedicated.

Peter Morey
London, 2025

Note on Editions and Terms

The following editions of Kamila Shamsie's novels have been used in this study, with the original date of publication in square brackets where this is different:

In the City by the Sea (London: Bloomsbury, 2004 [1998])
Salt and Saffron (Oxford: Oxford University Press, 2000)
Kartography (London: Bloomsbury, 2002)
Broken Verses (London: Bloomsbury, 2005)
Burnt Shadows (London: Bloomsbury, 2009)
A God in Every Stone (London and New Delhi: Bloomsbury, 2014)
Home Fire (London: Bloomsbury, 2017)
Best of Friends (London: Bloomsbury, 2022)

In the text, some words and names that appear in translation or which have been transliterated from non-English sources have different spellings. For example, Layla, the female lover from the tale of Layla and Majnun, is presented as Laila in some sources; likewise Majnun sometimes appears as Majnu. In the same way, *Mohajir* is sometimes rendered *Muhajir*. I have aimed to maintain a consistent spelling of these words except where I am quoting directly from sources that spell them differently.

Biographical Outline

1973   Kamila Shamsie born on 13 August in Karachi to Muneeza (née Habibullah) and Saleem Shamsie. Younger sister of Saman Shamsie, granddaughter of memoirist Jahanara Habibullah, and niece of the novelist Attia Hosain.

1977   Military coup in Pakistan sees the overthrow and subsequent execution of Prime Minister Zulfikar Ali Bhutto and the beginning of the dictatorship of General Zia ul-Haq. Repression of minorities and women's rights in his 'Islamisation' campaign. Shamsie joins the Karachi Grammar School, a selective co-educational day school, which she attends from kindergarten to A Levels at 18.

1979   Russian invasion of Afghanistan and beginning of armed resistance by fighters partly funded by the United States. One result is the influx of arms into Karachi and the exacerbation of existing tensions in the city. Hudood Ordinances introduced by Zia regime to replace the longstanding Pakistan Penal Code, a legacy of British rule, and implement Shariah law. Criminalises 'fornication' and adultery, and introduces punishments such as whipping, amputation, and stoning to death. The Zina provisions are particularly detrimental to women as they reduce their legal rights and the value of a woman's testimony.

1988   Death of General Zia in an unexplained plane explosion. Election of Benazir Bhutto, Pakistan's first woman prime minister.

1991   Shamsie enrols at Hamilton College, New York to pursue a BA in Creative Writing.

1994	Joins University of Massachusetts Amherst to study for an MFA under the tutelage of, among others, the Kashmiri poet Agha Shahid Ali.
1998	First novel, *In the City by the Sea*, published by Granta.
2000	Second novel, *Salt and Saffron*, published by Bloomsbury and Oxford University Press in Pakistan.
2001	11 September terror attacks in New York City, masterminded by the leadership of Al Qaeda. Beginning of so-called 'War on Terror'. Increased scrutiny and surveillance of Muslims around the world and especially in Western nations.
2002	USA and its allies invade Afghanistan. *Kartography* published by Bloomsbury.
2003	USA and Britain invade Iraq to depose the dictator Saddam Hussein.
2005	*Broken Verses* published by Bloomsbury.
2007	Shamsie takes up permanent residence in London. Benazir Bhutto assassinated by a suicide bomber at a political rally in December.
2009	*Burnt Shadows* published by Bloomsbury.
2011	Shamsie elected a Fellow of the Royal Society of Literature.
2012	Shamsie is granted indefinite leave to remain in the UK.
2013	Becomes a British citizen at a time when the Conservative government begins creating a 'hostile environment' for those in the UK without the correct legal status.
2014	*A God in Every Stone* published by Bloomsbury.
2016	Referendum in which the UK narrowly votes to leave the European Union.
2017	*Home Fire* published by Bloomsbury. Longlisted for Booker Prize (2017) and wins Women's Prize for Fiction (2018).
2019	Boris Johnson becomes British prime minister. The UK leaves the European Union. German Nelly Sachs prize award rescinded owing to Shamsie's support for the pro-Palestinian Boycott, Divestment and Sanctions (BDS) movement.
2022	*Best of Friends* published by Bloomsbury.

1.

Introduction: Transnational Writer of Pakistan

Kamila Shamsie is one of the most celebrated contemporary novelists writing in English. Her stories of people uprooted by history and politics, yet tenaciously clinging to those links that give meaning to their lives, have struck a chord with readers across the world. In novels that explore the power drives of colonialism and its consequences in the postcolonial present, Shamsie repeatedly investigates what it means to belong – to family, community, nation – when hostile forces are relentlessly tearing up the roots of such connections. Her characters find themselves displaced in a number of ways – physically, intellectually, emotionally – the effect of their upheavals being coloured by issues of race, class, and especially gender. Throughout her work, Shamsie includes strong women who often seek to strike back against injustice or, at the very least, find ways to accommodate change while trying to preserve deeply held principles. They attempt to carve out spaces of freedom in the face of pressures from powerful structures such as nationalism and patriarchy that sometimes reach across continents, laying claim to their allegiances and circumscribing their opportunities. Her protagonists are spirited individuals who recognise the institutional power ranged against them but fight on even so. Issues of autonomy, freedom, and the shadow of the past inform a body of work that cuts across time and space – from 1980s Pakistan (the country of her birth) to contemporary Britain and the United States, via Afghanistan, Turkey, Syria, and colonial India – yet whose concerns remain at all times uncompromisingly topical. The pressing challenges of today's world, to do with belonging, citizenship, women's rights, displacement, and the plight of asylum seekers and refugees, are addressed in fiction that is always testing the boundaries of the novel form in a restless quest to find new ways to frame these age-old problems.

Shamsie was born in Karachi, Pakistan in 1973 to a family with literature in the blood. She is the daughter of the renowned critic Muneeza Shamsie; granddaughter of the memoirist Jahanara Habibullah – whose record of courtly life in pre-Partition India, *Remembrance of Days Past: Glimpses of a Princely State*, influenced Shamsie's second and in some ways most personal novel, *Salt and Saffron* (2000); and great-niece of the novelist Attia Hosain, one of the foremost chroniclers of late-feudal India.[1] Her sister, Saman, is a successful children's writer. Traces of this dynasty of ground-breaking women can be seen in some of the preoccupations of Shamsie's fiction and, given such a background, it is unsurprising that her mother Muneeza recalls that 'Kamila was around eleven when she announced that she wanted to be a writer'.[2]

The legacies of violent historical upheavals, such as the Partition of India and Pakistan in 1947 and the Civil War of 1971 which led to the creation of Bangladesh, and their impact on women and children form the subject matter of Shamsie's early works. They have also marked her own family's journey from aristocratic feudal Indian landowners (or *Taluqdars*) under the Raj to modern Pakistani intellectuals. Like the principle dynasty in *Salt and Saffron*, the family was split by Partition, with some members staying in India and others migrating to the new homeland for Muslims, Pakistan, settling in Karachi. Muneeza Shamsie remembers childhood visits to her maternal grandmother in Lucknow, India and 'the Lucknow family house with its peeling paint, dark wood, coloured panes, white pillars and wide verandahs, tinted oval portraits and porcelain art nouveau shades. Then there were visits to the family village. The one-time ancestral mansion was but an unkempt tumbledown edifice yet held endless fascination for me'.[3] Something of this spirit of faded grandeur clings to several of Shamsie's early characters, emerging in a certain fastidiousness and class exclusivity, even when they have become urbane cosmopolitans.

After attending the co-educational Karachi Grammar School, Shamsie left Pakistan to study in the United States at Hamilton

INTRODUCTION

College and at the University of Massachusetts Amherst where she pursued creative writing under the renowned Indian–American poet and teacher Agha Shahid Ali, whose poetry provides one of the epigraphs for Shamsie's fifth novel, *Burnt Shadows* (2009), and whose influence is marked by the poetic feel for language evident in many of her works.[4] For several years, Shamsie moved between Pakistan, the United States, and Britain, before finally settling in London in 2007. She has since gained British citizenship, something which has affected her outlook and her writing in ways we will see when we come to examine her more recent novels.

Shamsie's first novel, *In the City by the Sea*, was published in 1998, and to date it has been followed by seven other novels, several short stories, journalistic forays, and a book on Pakistani history entitled *Offence: The Muslim Case*. Her work has garnered a number of international awards and prize nominations. In 2011 she was elected a Fellow of the Royal Society of Literature, while in 2013 she was among the novelists selected as Granta's '20 most promising young British authors under 40'.[5] Among her accolades are the Patras Bokhari Award from the Pakistan Academy of Letters for *Kartography* (2002), *Broken Verses* (2005), and *Best of Friends* (2023); the American Anisfield-Wolf Book and Danish ALOA awards and Italy's Boccaccio Prize for *Burnt Shadows* (2010); and the Women's Prize for Fiction 2018 for *Home Fire*. Controversy followed Shamsie's selection for the German Nelly Sachs Prize in 2019 when the awarding body became aware of her longstanding support for the pro-Palestinian Boycott, Divestment and Sanctions (BDS) movement against the Israeli state's policies towards the Palestinians in its midst. Despite backing for Shamsie from 250 distinguished writers including Arundhati Roy, Michael Ondaatje, and Sally Rooney, the award was rescinded.[6] Her stand on this issue is indicative of the commitment to justice and the ethical treatment of individuals and groups vulnerable to the agendas of dominant political interests that forms one of the central threads of her writing.

Many of Shamsie's novels are grounded in the familiar sights and sounds of Karachi and focus on family and inter-generational travails. As her career develops, however, there is a broadening out from the initial concentration on members of the Pakistani elite toward a more transnational focus in terms

3

of characters and themes. She includes perspectives from those marginalised by class and the effects of corruption, misapplied religion, and a Western-led global order that will stop at nothing to secure its aims. Whether they are citizens of countries whose development has been warped by colonial interventions, or migrants (or their offspring) living in Britain and the United States, Shamsie's characters are buffeted by the winds of war and geopolitics. What lends her work its unity is the acute attention paid to how the political intrudes upon the personal and has the power to shatter families and uproot friendships in its relentless onslaught. The complex legacies of empire run through the novels, becoming thematically dominant in more recent texts and, despite their often-strenuous efforts to avoid it, her characters are forced into a reckoning with decisions made by others in the past which restrict their lives in the present. As Bruce King puts it, in Shamsie's novels, '[t]o understand the present it is necessary to understand the past'.[7]

This challenge takes a particular shape in Pakistan, a nation born in the violent Partition from India when the British left in 1947. Pakistan was carved out of five provinces – Punjab, Sindh, Balochistan, North West Frontier Province, and East Bengal – as a homeland for Muslims who felt that their interests would not be safeguarded in predominantly Hindu India. This patchwork of different regions, ethnicities, and languages led to tensions; East Bengal, for instance, was geographically separate from the rest of the country, lying on the other side of neighbouring India and forming what was known as East Pakistan. Such diffuseness meant that, from the start, the religion of Islam took on a disproportionate importance in the forging of national identity, providing a glue with which to hold the nation together but, at the same time, diluting the pluralist vision of the nation's leader in the freedom struggle and first governor general after Independence, Muhammad Ali Jinnah.[8] The fissiparous tendencies of the heterogeneous group of regions that made up Pakistan came to a head in the general election of 1971, when the Awami League won a clear majority of seats in more populous East Pakistan, while the Pakistan People's Party, led by the new prime minister, Zulfikar Ali Bhutto, swept the board in the West. The Awami League's lack of a mandate in West Pakistan gave Bhutto and his backers in the army an excuse to refuse to recognise the result in the East. Military operations began to bring the province to heel, but fierce resistance escalated into a full-scale civil war during which around three million Bengalis were killed, culminating in the unconditional surrender of the Pakistan forces and the creation of the new independent nation of Bangladesh. The trauma of this second partition is felt most strongly in Shamsie's third novel, *Kartography*, where the war and its fallout are central to the plot.[9]

Relations between India and Pakistan have always been tense. Conflict over the state of Jammu and Kashmir, awarded to India at Partition but containing a Muslim majority populace, led to short-lived wars in 1947–48 and again in 1965, along with numerous skirmishes and stand-offs which continue to the present day. Matters were further complicated during the Cold War (1945–89), as superpower influence came decisively to shape postcolonial politics in both countries. Concerned at the non-aligned sympathies of India under Jawaharlal Nehru, which appeared to open the door to Soviet influence, the United States built strong ties with Pakistan which it viewed as strategically important, given its proximity to Afghanistan and the Soviet Union, while Pakistan in turn sought the additional security close relations with the Americans was felt to bring.[10] American support augmented the power of the military in Pakistan, who had been major players in the new nation's politics ever since the first military coup in 1958 when the president, Major General Iskander Ali Mirza, dismissed the elected civilian government and appointed General Ayub Khan to lead the country. Thus began the see-saw between civilian and military governments that has bedevilled Pakistan, further military coups taking place in 1971, 1977, and 1999. The army has continued to consolidate its power, cultivating an ever-growing portfolio of business interests, becoming a major landowner, and taking advantage of the ongoing privatisation programmes of successive governments to move into the finance, oil, and private security sectors.[11] Even when not in power itself, it is seen as a king-maker for the civilian parties, who are careful to do nothing to upset the army or act against its interests.

The United States further encouraged the proliferation of military power in the Cold War and, from the 1980s, backed this up with the requirement that the Pakistani economy be liberalised in line with the drive towards the privatisation of social and economic assets that was taking place in the West. During this time, it viewed Islam in particular as what Saadia Toor calls a 'bulwark against communism'.[12] Hence, there was an encouragement of conservative religious forces particularly after the Soviets invaded neighbouring Afghanistan in 1979. The anti-Soviet fight, conducted by volunteer combatants from all over the world, was portrayed as a *jihad*, a religious struggle. These fighters were referred to as *mujahideen*: soldiers for the faith. Ian Talbot notes how '[o]ne estimate puts the number of "foreigners" involved in the Afghan fighting as 35,000, drawn from 40 countries'.[13] Shamsie addresses the human and social cost of this influx into the region of men and arms in *Kartography* and *Burnt Shadows*.

After the Soviet withdrawal, the *mujahideen* was abandoned by its Western sponsors. Out of the subsequent turmoil in Afghanistan there eventually arose the Taliban, a Deobandi fundamentalist movement that took over the country, creating fertile ground for other groups such as Al Qaeda to establish their operations. The most infamous acts carried out by the latter were the attacks on the World Trade Center and Pentagon buildings in the United States on 11 September 2001. These atrocities and the United States' response to them set in train the so-called War on Terror wherein Muslims from all over the world found themselves the objects of suspicion and securitisation measures. Shamsie is one of the foremost chroniclers of the links in the historical chain which have led up to this moment: *Burnt Shadows*, for instance, explicitly draws connections between key global flashpoints since World War Two, showing how intolerance to others and their supposed expendability creates a world in which suspicion seems hardwired into nations and their policies towards other countries and their own minority communities.

The international crisis caused by the 1979 Soviet invasion of Afghanistan followed almost immediately after the coup in 1977 that brought General Zia ul-Haq to power in Pakistan. Zia is the bogeyman in several of Shamsie's novels where, like their author, characters grow up under his dictatorship in the 1980s. Zia executed his predecessor Bhutto, courted right-wing religious groups, and introduced repressive measures, tightening blasphemy laws, clamping down on minority rights, and curtailing the liberties of women. His so-called 'Islamisation' policies imposed strict Islamic dress expectations on women and discouraged their involvement in public activities. Most egregious was his imposition of Shariah legal principles which were particularly detrimental to women, removing safeguards and reducing their status in the eyes of the law. These discriminatory moves prompted an upsurge in resistance and the establishment of women's campaigning groups, most notably the Women's Action Forum. Shamsie dramatises the repressive dimensions of Zia's rule in her early novels with *In the City by the Sea* and *Broken Verses* engaging directly with the climate of fear created in the 1980s, but also showing female characters determined to fight back. Indeed, Shamsie's women are, time and again, the ones who take action against oppression and support others in doing so. Yaqoob and Hussain are right to claim that 'Shamsie champions women's autonomy by portraying socially rebellious, strong-willed and courageous women as her central characters', thereby contesting stereotypes which equate Pakistani women with 'passivity, self-sacrifice and endurance'.[14]

Following Zia's unexplained death in a plane explosion in 1988, democracy returned to Pakistan with the government of Benazir Bhutto. Shamsie's young women characters experience this as a time of liberation and optimism. However, Benazir and her successors Nawaz Sharif and General Pervaiz Musharraf were only partly able to roll back the worst excesses of the Zia era, so ingrained had the norms of the religious right become. Nonetheless, this seminal era and its strong women provide a model for resistance that is carried over into Shamsie's later work: for Aliya the convention-defying heroine of *Salt and Saffron*, read Zahra the human rights activist in *Best of Friends*; for Samina the feminist firebrand in *Broken Verses*, read Aneeka with her stand against the British state's forces of exclusion in *Home Fire* (2017). These women give a shape and impetus to Shamsie's critique of the way recent history has deformed the present and how grappling with its continuing legacy is both unavoidable and necessary.

After the 2001 terror attacks in the United States an atmosphere of widespread Islamophobia in the West created difficulties for Muslim minorities. Shamsie explores the effects of institutionalised prejudice and legalised xenophobia in *Home Fire* and *Best of Friends*. Here, Muslim characters discover that they exist in Britain only precariously, on sufferance so to speak, even if they have been born there. Citizenship – its safeguards, blind spots, and politicisation – becomes a key theme in these works. At the same time, the cultural curiosity that followed 9/11 meant that authors such as Shamsie found themselves caught up in a renewed interest among publishers and readers in work which appeared to illuminate the ways of Muslims and Muslim nations. Although she is a frequent contributor of articles to the liberal press in Britain, particularly the *Guardian* newspaper, Shamsie found herself increasingly uncomfortable with the expected role of spokesperson for Pakistan and for Muslims foisted on her in the War on Terror years. Describing her frustration with the pressure to take on a 'representative' role at this time, she comments: 'At first I was doing quite a lot of that and I wasn't a two-way intermediary. [My role] was to say to England or America, look, here is the more nuanced truth about the place I am from … After a while I pulled back from that because I didn't want to be pigeon-holed in that either and I am certainly not a spokesperson or representative'.[15] Although she continues to offer journalistic pieces on issues close to her heart, such as the status of refugees and asylum seekers, Shamsie prefers to explore urgent contemporary issues through fiction, dramatising moral complexities and decisions through characters who must push against the constraints of the present and the burden of the past within specific geographical contexts.[16]

The most pervasive location in Shamsie's work, where characters spend their formative years and whose influence continues to reverberate as they grow older and relocate to Britain or America, is the southern port city of Karachi. Karachi is more than just a place; it represents home, but also reveals how the ideal of home is always marked by contests around power and ownership. As such, Shamsie's Karachi epitomises the broader inclusions and exclusions of ethnic and national groups that form one of her key preoccupations. Although its origins go back to antiquity, Karachi was developed in the eighteenth century by Hindu merchants. It acted as a magnet for traders from all over the Subcontinent. It is now the economic powerhouse of Pakistan, accounting for twenty-five percent of Pakistan's gross domestic product, fifty-four percent of its tax revenue, and ninety-five percent of its international trade.[17] Karachi has always been a focus for economic migrants. The city grew in the nineteenth and twentieth centuries, but the biggest transformation occurred at Partition. Almost overnight the majority Hindu community was displaced and by 1951 ninety-six percent of the population was Muslim.[18] Karachi became Pakistan's first capital after Independence – only being supplanted by the new city of Islamabad in the 1960s – and drew a vast number of Partition migrants, or Mohajirs as they became known. This rapid change brought the newcomers into conflict with other groups such as the existing Sindhi population, with the more highly skilled and educated Mohajirs tending to monopolise the city's socio-economic assets. This led to a backlash and remedial efforts which in turn fostered a sense of Mohajir grievance. The 1970s and 1980s were disfigured by riots and the formation of ethnic political movements, such as the Mohajir Qaumi Movement (MQM) whose campaigns on behalf of the Urdu-speaking Mohajir population quickly took on paramilitary qualities. Rival armed groups sprang up in the 1980s, just in time to avail themselves of the armaments flooding into Karachi which were meant for the *mujahideen* fighting in Afghanistan.[19] Additionally, the rapid, unplanned expansion of the city as more and more incomers arrived, often setting up home in temporary encampments, easily outstripped the capacity of existing civic amenities such as electricity, water, and sewage systems. The gap was filled by criminal gangs, themselves often connected to political parties, who offered to supply what was missing – for a price.[20] Thus, the Karachi of Shamsie's novels is a place of danger as well as home, something most tangible in the pages of *Kartography*. Threats are always close at hand, sometimes a result of lawlessness and organised crime, but just as often emanating from vested interests and powerful elites mired in corruption and securing themselves through violence. (The same bullying by the powerful exposed in *In the City by the Sea* and *Kartography* is a constant undertone in *Best of Friends* too.)

One of the flashpoints in Karachi centred on the question of language, with riots in the early 1970s when the Sindh Assembly declared Sindhi to be the official language of the province alongside Urdu, the language of the Mohajirs.[21] Shamsie does not take sides in these disputes, instead preferring to encode some of the imaginative qualities and poetic richness of Urdu into her English-language novels. Indeed, the Urdu tradition provides a source of inspiration to Shamsie, mainly thanks to Agha Shahid Ali's tutelage. Yasmin Hameed has described how 'Urdu is a young but mature language' which 'flowered in the eighteenth and nineteenth centuries in the two major cultural centres' of Delhi and Lucknow. Over time, Urdu poetry – with its rich array of Persian-influenced forms, including the *ghazal* and the *nazm* – was pioneered by Mirza Ghalib (1797–1869), Altaf Hussain Hali (1837–1914), and the national poet of Pakistan, Muhammad Iqbal (1877–1938).[22] Unlike the West, where poetry tends to be a minority pursuit, Urdu poetry has broad popular and cross-class appeal in Pakistan.[23] Although claiming no special expertise, Shamsie is interested in how Urdu poetry in particular can open a path to alternative political visions. This is most noticeable in *Broken Verses*, with its doomed political poet, Omi, but throughout her work she is always keen to validate the life-worlds that Urdu encapsulates, but which are usually overlooked in English-language fiction. While Shamsie firmly rejects any notion that she might be a spokesperson for Pakistan, understanding of her work can be enriched by a familiarity with the other South Asian literary and linguistic traditions she invokes, such as the abundant currents of Urdu poetry or folk tales from Persian and Arabic. This multilingual literary inheritance manifests thematically in a fascination with the flexibility and nuances of different languages. In *Burnt Shadows*, characters note the changed emotional resonances offered by Urdu and English when trying to translate between the two tongues; they come to recognise that entering another language requires an openness to other cultures which militates against nativism and xenophobia. Although she writes in English, Shamsie is sensitive to the way in which perspectives are moulded by the power of languages to modulate experience. The characters with whom we are invited to identify most strongly in her works are those who reach across barriers of language, culture, and nation to make connections with others.

Pakistan, and particularly Karachi, provides the lodestar in Shamsie's work, guiding and influencing choices and attitudes even when characters live far away. Yet, the fact that Shamsie writes in English, coupled with her 2007 relocation to London, mean that it would be wrong simply to pigeonhole her as a representative Pakistani writer, whatever that phrase may mean. Many successful writers choose to live in Pakistan and write in its indigenous languages such as Punjabi, Sindhi, Pashto, and Balochi. At the same time, it is possible to argue for English itself as a Pakistani language given its history and ubiquity, particularly among the middle class. The novelist Bina Shah claims as much when she praises English's 'directness and precision'. She says, 'English is a practical choice for the writers of my generation: it's a global language, one that makes us immediately accessible to international readers without having to go through the pain and inconvenience of translation'.[24] In these terms, location and language choice are only part of what connects a writer to a particular place. Sabyn Javeri prefers a more inclusive approach when she categorises as a Pakistani writer 'one who feels a connection to the land either by origin or by sensibility'.[25] It is certainly important that as wide a variety of writers as possible from formerly colonised nations are heard and there is some distance to go before the global publishing industry sheds its class and ethnic biases towards certain types of voice and subject matter. Rather than shackling contemporary English-language writers like Shamsie as spokespersons for a nation, it might be more useful to follow Gohar Karim Khan's lead and understand contemporary anglophone Pakistani literature as a cultural contact zone of exchange, caught up in a global market for books and ideas.[26] There may be compromises involved in embracing this position, but there are also opportunities. Shamsie is aware of the potential and pitfalls of her role and incorporates an acknowledgement of them into her work.

When one considers her move to live in Britain, her dual nationality, and the increasingly international scope of her fictions, it might now be more accurate to describe Shamsie as a transnational writer of Pakistan. In an interview in 2018, she observed: 'The idea of the nation-state as the defining framework of a novel has less and less relevance in this interconnected world. At the very least, I seem to have become incapable of imagining a novel that is restricted within the boundaries of a single nation'.[27] This credo of imaginative openness to thinking across borders might lead us to consider what it means to be a transnational writer, and to produce transnational writing in the modern, post-9/11 world. In his introduction to *Transnational Literature*, Paul Jay defines his object of study as 'a particular type of literature, emergent at an identifiable historical moment and dealing ... with a set of issues and themes associated with decolonisation, globalisation, postmodernity, and technology'.[28] The category develops in response to an increasing porousness of national borders and often explores themes of migration and exile. It has bred a generation of writers who, says Jay, are '[m]obile, well-educated and savvy about the uses of social media' and whose work focuses on 'stories of dispossession and displacement, using the resources of fiction, poetry and drama to complicate narratives of settlement and progress'.[29] Such texts are often formally experimental. Moreover, the sheer proliferation of narratives enabled by new media forms ensures that the stranglehold of hegemonic national discourses can never be complete. The circulation of stories and genres across the world means that literature is always already transnational and – through quotation, reference, and allusion – intertextuality becomes synonymous with mobility and the crossing of borders.

The themes and techniques in Shamsie's recent fiction show how transnationalism becomes an ethical standpoint resulting in the development of a distinct intertextual aesthetic to place against what Chimamanda Ngozi Adichie has called the tyranny of 'the single story'.[30] In this aesthetic, intertextuality – in the form of heightened mythic realism, hyper-performativity, and the judicious use of framing texts such as Sophocles' *Antigone* and the landmark works of colonial fiction – are employed to shatter the complacency (and often verbosity) of authoritative narratives which crowd out the voices of those who continue to suffer most from colonialism's legacy of inequality. We might update one aspect of Jay's description, though, since the porousness of borders has, in recent years, been countered by a populist backlash resulting in a tightening of national entry conditions and a desire to mark out and even expel those 'unwelcome' migrants or supposedly disloyal subjects.

It is this backlash that feeds the fire in Shamsie's most recent novels, several of which are concerned with the question of the citizenship rights of minorities.

Finally, transnational literature is marked by a concern with history and who gets to write it, its works being imbued with a commitment to present often-neglected voices and interrogate established centre–periphery binaries. This concern with the effects of history on the individual and whose story is worth recording is one of the hallmarks of Shamsie's fiction. It shares with the work of her contemporaries, such as Elif Shafak and Ahdaf Soueif, a historically informed cosmopolitanism in which multiple focalisation introduces a range of perspectives reflecting a principled internationalism. Shamsie's brand of transnational writing increasingly takes as its subject matter the experiences of characters who have themselves crossed borders, often in situations where globalised economic, political, and military forces decisively affect the fate of those with Muslim backgrounds. In her writing, the power of the nation is often seen to be unwelcoming, making the lives of citizens with transnational kinship networks and affiliations more hazardous. Shamsie's novels share the preoccupation of much fiction produced in the years since the 11 September 2001 terror attacks on the United States and the subsequent declaration of a 'War on Terror'. In this work the vast securitisation network brought to bear to track, trace, discipline, and sometimes deport Muslim subjects in the West becomes the focal point. Such writing is transnational because it captures some of the effects of that resurgent nationalism on Muslim subjects whose status in Western countries can now more easily be called into question. Yet Shamsie's novels in particular have a pressing interest in showing how the recent constraining developments for Muslims were not brought spontaneously into being by 9/11 but are a continuation of historical forces and attitudes traceable to the age of the great European empires in the nineteenth and early twentieth centuries.

As a writer who has moved across national borders and who is now a citizen of a country 4,000 miles away from her place of birth, Shamsie is, in biographical terms, clearly a transnational subject. Moreover, as a successful writer in a global literary marketplace, she and her works are also positioned within transnational networks of production, circulation, and evaluation which decisively shape her novels and their reception. Writing of English literature in the world today, Rebecca Walkowitz notes how, in an age of globalisation, contemporary literature is, 'in many ways, a comparative literature: works circulate in several literary systems at once and can – some would say need – to be read within several national traditions'.[31] One of the distinctive qualities of Shamsie's novels is their unflinching determination to embrace the challenge of bringing together traditions and outlooks which current political orthodoxy often implies are incompatible. History here is not so much linear as intermeshed. At its heart are those people who think or move in ways that test permissible boundaries in search of freedom. Walter Benjamin famously described what he called the Angel of History:

> His face is turned toward the past. Where we perceive a chain of events, he sees one single catastrophe which keeps piling wreckage upon wreckage and hurls it in front of his feet. The angel would like to stay, awaken the dead, and make whole what has been smashed. But a storm is blowing from Paradise; it has got caught in his wings with such violence that the angel can no longer close them. This storm irresistibly propels him into the future to which his back is turned, while the pile of debris before him grows skyward.[32]

In the eye of the hurricane of history that uproots them and scatters them across the globe, Shamsie's characters inch forward through the wreckage of past and present, gathering their strength and turning to face the future.

2.

Early Works: *In the City by the Sea* and *Salt and Saffron*

In the City by the Sea (1998) marks the start of Shamsie's career-long investigation into family dynamics and their relation to historical forces. It was submitted for assessment as her MFA thesis at Amherst. Her first novel is governed by the child's-eye point of view of Hasan, the cricket-mad son of a prominent family. Hasan finds his world turned upside down and his sense of security shattered by two events: witnessing a young neighbour's fatal fall from his roof while flying a kite; and the arrest of his Uncle Salman, a popular anti-corruption politician who has fallen foul of the county's new military rulers.[1] Hasan has gradually to come to terms with sudden, irrevocable change, symbolised most potently by the boy's death but brought even closer to home by the imprisonment and potential execution of Salman.

Hasan is the first of those Shamsie protagonists who find themselves on the cusp of the change from childhood or youth to the world of adult preoccupations. The novel is shaped by his attempts to make sense of adult events. With his protective fantasies drawn from tales of dragon-slaying knights and superheroes, Hasan initiates the line of Shamsie characters who prefer to take solace in illusion or self-deception when the world turns hostile. This tendency is repeated in later novels with older protagonists too, where a situation and its implications often remain clouded by wish-fulfilment or a refusal to face facts. Yet, for all these cocooning efforts, the realities of political power and human mortality in the end prove unavoidable.

In the City by the Sea is also the first of Shamsie's explorations into the effects of corruption and tyranny. In spite of their domestic settings, history does not go on safely outside her stories, it enters by force, violently, sweeping away central characters as it passes. In this novel, the net closes around Uncle Salman, first in the form of house arrest and thereafter through imprisonment and an impending trial for treason, a charge carrying the likely punishment of death. Salman's fate becomes linked to that of Azeem, the kite-flying neighbour, as Hasan tries to process these two modes by which a life may be extinguished – chance and human malevolence. Indeed, for much of the novel he studiously avoids allowing himself to confront the memory of Azeem's death plunge – its horror is sublimated through images of bursting bubbles or splitting fruit and the splatter of their juices. Even so, the novel circles back to this traumatic incident, belying Hasan's mental attempts to euphemise it. Such avoidance is part of his coping mechanism: when Hasan asks another uncle, Latif, how someone may escape death he receives the less-than-comforting response that 'Escape is OOQ ... Out of Question ... Avoidance, however, might be achieved for very many years' (*In the City by the Sea*, 117). Another way is to seek refuge in the ordered rituals of a cricket match or stealing at night through the familiar shadows of his home where everything stays in place.

Faced with Uncle Salman's incarceration and uncertain fate, Hasan seeks a way to end his family's torment. He takes refuge in a fantasy world where he is the hero of a chivalric quest to save his uncle and defeat the forces of evil, embodied by the country's president. Along the way he draws on the advice of Latif, his daughter Zehra – the object of Hasan's nascent affections – and the crepuscular Oldest Man, a gnomic storyteller who in his longevity appears able to elude death and who declares freedom of spirit to be the best weapon. Inspired by their advice, Hasan develops elaborate plans whereby he will bring about the overthrow of the president and rescue his uncle. As each one proves impractical Hasan awakens to the same sense of impotence experienced by the adults of the family: the gnawing dread and sense of inevitable doom that comes to pervade the text until almost the very end.

Although the characters populating *In the City by the Sea* are drawn from a recognisable world of modern political intrigue, aspects of the fantasy story come to bleed into real-world events too. The novel maintains a realist societal framework, but many of its elements have a slightly hazy, fabular quality not solely attributable to Hasan's romanticising. This effect is augmented by the decision not to name certain places and characters despite the setting obviously being a very thinly veiled version of Pakistan; the City by the Sea is recognisably the Karachi that will come to dominate Shamsie's early novels; while the president is clearly modelled on 1980s Pakistani dictator Zia ul-Haq, right down to his 'hollow' eyes and 'boot-polish moustache'. Another unnamed character is the Widow, a relative who comes to reside next door with Uncle Latif. She is described as 'all fire and brilliance' (127) and seems almost to exist at the border between the waking and sleeping worlds. When taxed by Hasan about the nature of death, the Widow responds that it is '[j]ust a change in location. A movement from this world to the land bordering sleep'. She feels a strong connection with her dead husband and treasures a feather pillow he was buying for her when he collapsed and died, claiming it allows her to retain a mystical connection with him: when all its feathers are gone, she says, she will join him. While the Widow indulges the childish fantasies of Hasan, desperate to find a figure on whom to project the ability to right the wrong done to his family, she does seem gifted with the charisma and vision to transcend the grim political realities and operate on a level where she becomes a symbol of democracy and hope. The Widow turns out to be a feminist activist who, with her Bodyguard – an ever-changing entourage formed by those whom society has rejected – stages rescue missions for other widows who have fallen prey to the attempts of male relatives to bully, cajole, or threaten them into signing away their late husbands' property. Hasan and Zehra imagine her as a superhero bearing down on male miscreants to ensure justice: momentarily mixing up his fantasy narratives, the punning Hasan excitedly sings, 'We hear she is a Wiz of a Wid if ever a Wid there was' (175). The Widow is the first of many characteristically strong Shamsie women.[2] Here, she is joined by Hasan's mother and Gul Mumani, Salman's wife, who keep the family together in the face of almost intolerable external pressures. At the end, reflecting the new spirit of optimism that accompanies the demise of the dictator Zia and the arrival of Pakistan's first woman prime minister, Benazir

Bhutto, the Widow announces political plans: she may join Salman's party, form one of her own, or create a non-government organisation to campaign and hold to account those in power. The main male figures in the novel are rendered notably impotent by events, for all their putative social standing in this patriarchal country. Salman is 'the saviour of the nation', a highly popular anti-corruption political leader whose ascent to high office is abruptly reversed by the coup which has brought the president and his military henchmen to power. He comes from a family of politicians – an uncle was himself an imprisoned freedom fighter who later became prime minister. When he is arrested, Salman's many followers organise strikes and protests that bring the City by the Sea to a halt. They scatter pine cones as a symbol of resistance, sending a daily shower of them into the compound of Salman's residence. Yet, for all his popular backing and the devotion he provokes in his nephew, Salman seems an oddly indecisive character with a certain scepticism about the effectiveness of democracy for the society he would, nonetheless, lead. Hasan's father, Aba, himself a lawyer who has now fallen foul of the regime and can no longer practise, describes the difference between his own pragmatic and Salman's more uncompromising view, as having to do with the nature of time:

> 'For Salman, time is pendular ... That's why he's such a nostalgist, always talking about his uncle's glorious governance. See, to Salman, nostalgia is hope; to me, it's usually loss. Linear time, that's my view. ... Given Salman's situation, my belief in linear time gives me hope ... Situations don't have to keep recurring. It's just that people generally have such limited imaginations that originality seldom occurs'. (103–104)

Here we find an early articulation of the characteristic Shamsiean interest in how characters understand and relate to the past. David Waterman has noted how the image of pendular time captures the apparent destiny of Karachi (and Pakistan more generally) going through seemingly endless 'cycles of political crises which give the impression of a present concurrent with its recent past ... Pendular time is linked very early to homecoming, nostalgia, escape, [and] immobility'.[3] The tension between fate and action is a persistent theme in the novel, linking the dilemmas of the adults who find themselves at the mercy of an impervious politico-military force with Hasan's frustrated desire to act decisively to enforce the 'happy ever after' denouement familiar from childhood stories.

Aba continues his optimistic train of thought, concluding 'So what if there are no precedents for a completely happy ending' (104). Upon reaching the end of the novel, and seeing Salman rescued by an implausible change of heart among the ruling generals resulting in the president being sent into exile, it is tempting think that Aba (and Shamsie) is here preparing us for a determinedly upbeat conclusion which cuts sharply against the preceding direction of travel. Everything is prepared for Salman to meet the same fate as Pakistan's revered Prime Minister Zulfikar Ali Bhutto, hanged by Zia ul-Haq in the coup of 1979. Instead, the fantasy world resurfaces again to pluck Salman almost from the hangman's noose when a sudden and unexplained coup unseats the president and Salman is set free. Shamsie's later work increasingly rejects such upbeat endings where problems are simply wished away. There is also, at this early stage, a certain reluctance to move beyond the world of the wealthy elite to take the temperature of the country at large. We inhabit the houses of the rich, go to their parties and ceremonies, and travel with Hasan in a military convoy that escorts him on a day out to the beach. By contrast, the lives of the 'other half' – the poor, the destitute, and the servant class – are kept at a distance. Shamsie is aware of their existence and Hasan is involved in a stand-off with a beggar girl when, for once, he leaves the luxury of his air-conditioned, chauffeur-driven car (39). But there is as yet no concerted effort to 'get inside' the experience of the less fortunate. The broadening of Shamsie's social horizons is one of the key developments in her later fiction, which will eventually give us memorable characters such as the Afghan taxi-driving refugee Abdullah in *Burnt Shadows*, the working-class Pasha family in *Home Fire*, and the beleaguered deportee Azam in *Best of Friends*.

*

Shamsie's second novel, *Salt and Saffron* (2000), treats storytelling as a theme at the same time as it performs the selections, omissions, revisions, and what the text calls 'remembered biases' by which we construct the narratives of our lives and those of our families. Shamsie's early plots frequently circle around mysteries, family secrets and the fallout when they are discovered. In *Salt and Saffron* a family mystery is at the heart of the text: what has happened to the protagonist Aliya's second cousin Mariam, who has shocked their aristocratic family, the Dard-e-Dils, by eloping with its cook? This essentially comic story is partly in dialogue with a novel from 1961 written by Shamsie's aunt, Attia Hosain: *Sunlight on a Broken Column*. Both texts share an interest in the travails of the feudal aristocracy in a changing Subcontinent, their obsessive concern for 'lineage', and the challenges wrought by generational conflicts and the desire for freedom.[4] The Dard-e-Dils (whose name – in a nod to the nineteenth-century Persian/Urdu poet Ghalib – means 'Aching Heart') can trace their family history back to the days of the Mughal Empire and have maintained their status through strategic alliances, yet now are split between a branch that has opted for Pakistan in 1947 and another that has stayed in India.

Our acerbic, Western-educated narrator, Aliya, is the first of those Shamsie characters displaying what Rehana Ahmed has called 'elite cosmopolitanism'.[5] She first appears sharing her family's colourful history with a handsome passenger on a transatlantic flight from the US to Britain. Thereafter, this sharp-witted young woman is our guide on a journey that takes us from the West back to Pakistan and through centuries of family myth and legend from the pre-Mughal period to the end of the millennium. The Dard-e-Dil family story maps closely onto that of South Asia in the last 500 years. The novel has a loose, looping structure, shaped by Aliya's powers of recall and narrative verve, which slides between the present moment and stories from the past. It is, at the same time, a dynastic epic, a love story, a social satire on the Pakistani elite, and a national allegory in the Jamesonian sense whereby the fates of individual characters can be mapped onto that of the nation of which they are part.[6] The Dard-e-Dils have been involved in all the major events which have shaped the Subcontinent: their ancestral home in India has been an independent fiefdom, part of the Mughal Empire, and was annexed by the British after the 1857 Rebellion. More recently, the family has been torn apart by the decision of its two patriarchs, Akbar and Sulaiman, to declare for Pakistan and India respectively at Partition in 1947. A third brother, Taimur, rebels against the stifling snobbery of his family and strikes out on his own, never to be heard from again. Years later, however, on the day of Aliya's birth, a taciturn woman claiming to be his daughter, Mariam, appears and is taken into the family home, now in Karachi.

Aliya's efforts to make sense of the tangled legacy of the Dard-e-Dils take a turn when Mariam, with whom she has become close, elopes with the family cook, Masood: their cross-class liaison provoking scandalised horror among the status-conscious family. But the Dard-e-Dils' outraged concern for respectability and purity is slowly revealed to be an illusion as Aliya learns more about instances of illegitimacy that have peppered the family history, and the unconventional choices of female members who have chafed against socially restrictive conventions. Aliya's grandmother Abida Dadi turns out to have been a one-time Marxist, and her Aunt Meher is having an affair with a married banker in Greece and has taught herself to fly planes while living abroad. Some have been drawn back into a kind of orthodoxy but others, like Mariam, have moved to foreign lands to start afresh. In each case, however, their fortitude and energy provide opportunities for new stories to be forged. Their examples only slowly begin to resonate with Aliya as she is increasingly taken up with the mysterious fate of Mariam and Masood who, like Taimur, have disappeared into the realms of a family cautionary tale. Aliya's fascination with this cross-class love affair is in part because she herself is romantically drawn to her charming fellow airline passenger, Khaleel, who resurfaces later but who, it transpires, comes from a poor district of Karachi and thus will never be accepted by the Dard-e-Dils. The story comes to be about Aliya's discovery, not so much of the secrets and fate of Mariam and Masood, but of her own power to flout convention in the pursuit of love.[7] To do so she must overcome her in-built snobbery, the product of wealth and an expensive international education which has given her cosmopolitan tastes but also a tendency to sneering superiority and a fondness for copious quotations and name-dropping of figures from the high cultures of Europe and South Asia.

The socially frustrated lovers Aliya and Khaleel, like Mariam and Masood, are 'not-quite pairs': unconventional duos of one kind or another whose appearance is said, in family lore, to herald disaster for the Dard-e-Dils. Although in legend such duos tend to be male, Aliya comes to realise that she and Mariam also form such a pair. Where Aliya is garrulous, Mariam is silent. Their closeness allows her to translate the wordless Mariam's language of gesture which, it is suggested, gives her a way of parodying and subverting patriarchal demands that the good Pakistani woman be silent and submissive. When Mariam refuses to speak at all, Aliya's father suggests that 'she's taking the notion of a woman's traditional role a little too literally' (*Salt and Saffron*, 131), while Aliya herself ponders whether 'Mariam's silence was a protest against the prejudice built into language' (214). In discovering more of Mariam's story, Aliya recognises their affinity and on the last page, as she gazes out from Mariam's room on the hibiscus her beloved aunt planted in the garden, she verbalises the connection, observing how 'the glass between it and me was both a window and a mirror' (244).[8] In an interesting psychoanalytic reading of the novel, Khan Touseef Osman notes how Aliya is trapped by the social stratification built into what he calls a 'familial metanarrative' of aristocratic exceptionalism that narrows her own choices. This is reflected on the level of form too, as 'it is very apparent that Aliya is a narrator with personal prejudices and limitations of knowledge. This is consistent with the theme of the novel that represents the evolution of her character from a biased perspective to free-thinking and from ignorance to knowledge'.[9]

As Aliya begins to understand the limitations of her pampered worldview she comes to see the often-arbitrary nature of invented bloodlines and the tenuous meaning of legitimacy. Rebelling against the complacent arrogance that marks the feudalistic paternalism embodied by her set, she nonetheless discovers the difficulty of shaking off her own learned snobbery: slowly becoming more conscious of her instinctive childhood aversion to the unwashed children of her Ayah with whom she played and having to overcome an ingrained feeling of 'disgust' when she first hears the news of Mariam's elopement with a lowly servant. Yet, rather than air-brushing renegades such as Mariam out of the family story, as would her gossipy but starchy aunts,

Aliya learns that '[n]o star, except the brightest, has meaning on its own' (130). Meaning is provided by context; to 'say that our family was involved in battles and treaties, patronized poetry and dance, was sometimes generous and sometimes cruel ... is not enough. You have to isolate each life, have to say that here lies the first discordant note and look how it is echoed in this life and see the discordance transformed into a necessary part of the whole' (117). To simply live in and through the family's grandiloquent myths of itself is not enough. Aliya comes to see that 'when we tell our stories our stories tell on us; they reveal what is and is not explicable in our lives' (242). To tell stories is to cook up coherence out of contingency using many ingredients, just as Masood the wonder-cook once produced sumptuous meals for the family before disgracefully running away with one of its female members. Aliya reflects on '[h]ow the absence of a single ingredient can alter the meal before you. How the absence of a detail can alter a story. How much salt had been left out in all the stories I'd heard from, and about, my family? How much salt did I leave out when I turned my memories of Mariam and Masood into a story?' (179).

Salt and Saffron contains several of those ingredients that will be combined with their own increasingly mouth-watering results in Shamsie's later works. There are word-plays and puns aplenty; a preoccupation with storytelling; a hybrid cultural inheritance formed by a cosmopolitan education and manifest in concern for the different emotional resonances of Urdu and English; and consciousness of the destructive force of a sense of class and the role of inherited traits. Typical of the early novels is the role played by Karachi itself. The city by the sea is introduced as a brash, brightly lit cosmopolis where affluence and poverty live side-by-side. (At one point, Aliya and her cousin Sameer take a walk along the eclectic public space of Clifton Beach discussing the mystery of Mariam and Masood, their conversation all along accompanied by the counterpoint provided by an importunate beggar.) It is also a place of corruption, where wealth and status count for more than the law: Ayah's son-in-law has died in police custody, leaving her to strive for the income necessary to send her granddaughter to school, while Aliya is able to bribe a traffic cop and avoid going to court for running a red light in her car.

Quratulain Shirazi describes *Salt and Saffron* as 'an effective endeavour to reconcile the competing forces of globalization and localization, tradition and modernity, and past and present. The novel is innovative and fresh in its approach and treatment as it playfully revisits the past traditions and conceptions and rejects them as irrelevant'.[10] However, in some of its elements the novel has not yet escaped the gravitational pull of one of its main literary precursors. The numerous echoes of Salman Rushdie's *Midnight's Children*, with its digressions and self-conscious interruptions to the narrative – along with three characters who are midnight-born, an interfering midwife, and symbolic correspondences between storytelling and cooking – combine with the heavy-handed allegorical correspondences between the Dard-e-Dils and the fates of India and Pakistan to give *Salt and Saffron* a slightly derivative feel.[11] Finally, in contrast to the satisfying ambiguity of later novels where a degree of indeterminacy sustains our interest in characters to the end (and beyond) – Raza disappearing into the netherworld of Guantanamo Bay at the end of *Burnt Shadows*, or the uncertain long-term psychological cost of Aasmaani's fixation with the doomed lovers in *Broken Verses* – in *Salt and Saffron* Shamsie strongly hints at a conventional romantic denouement as Aliya and Khaleel are united and a happy ending abroad is concocted for Mariam and Masood too. The darker Shamsiean worldview, in which characters appear as powerless creatures at risk of being crushed beneath the wheels of geopolitics and history, has yet to emerge.

3.

Echoes of the Past: *Kartography* and *Broken Verses*

Aliya and Mariam are the first of Shamsie's 'not-quite pairs': figures who are often siblings or cousins, but sometimes simply kindred spirits. Such figures start off with strong bonds which are thereafter worn away by external pressures, leading to what Caroline Herbert has termed a 'tension between strangeness and intimacy'.[1] In Shamsie's next novel, *Kartography* (2002), two adolescent Karachiites – Raheen and Karim – are at first inseparable friends with an almost psychic connection that expresses itself through their love of puns, wordplay, and an ear for linguistic incongruity that evolves into a whole shared way of seeing the city and its people. Karachi in the 1980s is explored in all its teeming multiplicity: a site of youthful bonds and hijinks, burgeoning sexual awareness, shared experiences and memories; but a metropolis also increasingly torn apart by violence and ethnic tensions. As time goes on, forces from the past re-emerge to drive a wedge between the two young protagonists.

A concern for the impact of past injustices on the present is often reflected in the dual time signatures of Shamsie's novels: plot lines are split and the narrative switches between 'then' and 'now' as a way of gesturing towards historical connectivity. To understand the present, protagonists must come to a clearer vision of the past. Raheen's and Karim's parents form a foursome during the duo's childhood, but Karim's father, Ali's decision to move abroad with his family as lawlessness spreads through the city serves to uncover longstanding tensions dating back to 1971 and the Civil War that lead to the creation of Bangladesh from what was East Pakistan.

Shamsie has noted how the 1971 war has become a blank space in the history of Pakistan: a defeat too painful to reflect upon. She comments: 'If there is one period in history from which Pakistan most adamantly averts its eyes, it is 1971', what she describes as 'that blood-soaked epoch'.[2] Shamsie's determination to force an account with history to explain strife in the present here takes place through memory: the suppressed memories of the older generation unexpectedly weigh on the lived realities of the younger characters in a Karachi caught up in a seemingly endless cycle of violence. The Bhutto government's refusal to respect the election result in the then East Pakistan which gave the Awami League a resounding victory, and the disastrous decision to try to enforce the will of the West Pakistan elite through military means, split the already fragmented nation and unleashed the demons of racial prejudice. In *Kartography*, Shamsie maps these macro-political developments onto the relationships of the main protagonists' parents at the time, while also exploring the way ongoing injustices in the present are affected by a battle for pre-eminence which has class as well as ethnic dimensions.

The novel moves between these two contexts: the late 1980s to mid-1990s – as Raheen and Karim's lives take them away from Karachi and from each other – and 1971, when fateful decisions were made and bonds of love crushed by the weight of nationalist bigotry. We are made aware at the start that Ali's wife (and Karim's mother), Maheen, was originally engaged to be married to Raheen's father, Zafar. Ali himself was at that time close to Yasmin, who ends up as Zafar's wife and Raheen's mother. The novel slowly reveals the circumstances under which their partner-swap took place and how Zafar and Maheen's engagement was broken off at the time of the war. Maheen is a Bengali while Zafar is a Mohajir: one of those many thousands of refugees who left India at Partition to make a home in West Pakistan's principle cities, among them Karachi. In time, the Mohajirs have become the established majority, enjoying an elite status with all the social and economic advantages that come with it, confining other groups, such as the Sindhis who lived in Karachi before 1947, to a secondary status, although now this hegemony is coming under pressure. The situation for Bengalis like Maheen is even worse, with anti-Bengali sentiment rife and the polarisation of the war leading friends and colleagues to turn against Zafar and his intended bride. In circumstances that expose his motives as ambiguous, Zafar renounces Maheen, thereby surrendering to the ethnic nationalism and racism that have gripped the country. He discovers that even in love one cannot escape the forces of history. After the war, Ali and Maheen marry instead but, despite the birth of Karim, their union is not a happy one and they migrate to the United States before divorcing.

The ethnic animosity that has forced apart Zafar and Maheen is a precursor to tensions in mid-1980s Karachi where the running sore of hostility between the Mohajir and Sindhi populations has resulted in huge inequalities in wealth, the creation of ethnically based political parties such as the Mohajir Qaumi Movement (MQM), gangsterism, and an upsurge of violence which makes parts of the city into no-go areas. Despite their comfortable backgrounds, Raheen and Karim are exposed to the prevailing atmosphere of hostility when they leave their homes in the comparative safety of the luxurious Clifton area. Raheen notes the deterioration of Karachi and when she too leaves to study in America her attempts to preserve an image of her beloved home city come into conflict with Karim's more sanguine, less romanticised view, expressed in the way he returns her anodyne letters to him in cut-up, rearranged form. Karim's passion for mapmaking, which gives the novel its punning title, begins as an effort to retain the emotional core of the city he is about to leave behind, and he gifts Raheen a hand-drawn map of Karachi filled with reflections of remembered places and incidents from their youth. Yet time and physical distance lead him to understand something it takes Raheen longer to learn: that the city of their youth is hopelessly split by class and ethnic schisms which have decisively shaped their own life stories, and that 'when you have seen the sorrows of the rest of the world you can't go on pretending none of it matters' (*Kartography*, 141). Karim's cartography comes to be about commemorating the experiences of Karachi, including the violence that has defaced what the press call 'DEATH CITY' (147), while Raheen prefers the seemingly safer streets of the more affluent Clifton district.

In their different ways of attempting to fix the city, Raheen sees the pair as reproducing the dichotomous understandings of geography traceable to the Greek polymaths Eratosthenes and Strabo. Eratosthenes – the 'grandfather of cartography' (180) – is taken to herald a more literalist understanding of mapping when his approach is compared with the descriptive, evocative geography of Strabo for whom, as with Homer, the spirit of a place is its most salient feature. (Raheen even writes a short Italo Calvino pastiche, entitled *Envisionable Cities*, to articulate her sense of the powerful connection between place and imagination.) It is only after a series of brushes with the violent, inequitable realities of the city that Raheen is reconciled to her childhood friend's view of the need to face up to the consequences of the past in the here and now. Karim's mapmaking is spurred by the desire to find a non-hierarchical way to record and give shape to the lived realities of a city which is, as Cara Cilano has put it (quoting Edward Soja), '"discontinuous, fragmented, polycentric"'.[3] Although they cannot undo the sins of the past, Raheen and Karim end by agreeing the need to create an interactive map of Karachi containing links to images and sound files that users can augment in order to come closer to capturing the essence of the city and bridge what the novel calls 'the difference between copying an image and interpreting a soul' (163):

> You start with a basic street map, OK, but everywhere there are links. Click here, you get sound files of Karachiites telling stories of what it's like to live in different parts of town. Click there, you get a visual of a particular street ... Click, you hear a poem. Click, you see a painting. Choice of languages in which you can read the thing. Sound files in all kinds of dialects. Strong on graphics for people who are illiterate. (337)

This alternative evolving multimedia cartographical record will form an archive allowing the city's diversity to express itself through the shared memories and identifications of its varied populace. It is at once an organic social document and a testament to the divisions that have decisively shaped the city's story and which resonate across the decades. As such, it embodies Stuart Hall's injunction that the development of any such community archive must be 'an on-going, never completed project'. Hall says, 'Archives ... stand in an active, dialogic, relation to the questions which the present puts to the past; and the present always puts its questions differently from one generation to another'.[4] Shamsie herself has noted how '[m]aps have an imperial aspect, because historically they've assisted in invasions, territorial acquisition, and trade. I was excited during the research for *Kartography* when I discovered that originally maps were considered to belong more to the world of literature than geography or science, because they are used to illustrate stories. I hope through my novels to create different story-maps on Karachi'.[5] In its form too, *Kartography* reproduces these intertextual ideals, as Caroline Herbert observes: 'Shamsie draws in non-narrative forms to complicate linearity. Raheen's narration is interrupted by other voices and texts, such as Karim's maps, letters, her creative writing assignments, and the parents' testimonies of 1971'.[6] As such, *Kartography* anticipates the collage technique which will become a key feature of *Home Fire* fifteen years later.

In comparison to our brief insights into the precariousness of those living in poverty on the margins, the tribulations of the elite, and in particular their complicated love lives, are played out in detail. They connect the generation of the Civil War with Raheen's friends in the 1980s who are also subject to frustrated love and kept apart by social distinctions as the novel explores the interstices of friendship and love. Raheen loves Karim but feels stirrings of sexual desire for the dashing Zia (whose well-connected family are rich enough to provide him with an annexe to the family home complete with its own bar!). Zia, in turn, is smitten by their even-richer friend Sonia who hails from a new-money background and whose increasing conservatism of dress and habit reflects the Islamisation campaign that marked the 1980s in Pakistan.[7] When it is arranged that Sonia will marry an eligible suitor, Zia's father – at the behest of his jealous son – exploits his connections to discredit Sonia's father by implying he is connected to the drug trade. The ensuing broken engagement and social shame endured by Sonia replays the fate of Maheen when former friends turn on her and Zafar in 1971.

The temporal echoes and dual stories of entangled couples, along with a pervasive sense of ethnic and class tension blighting Pakistan and ready to erupt at any time, provide the structural and thematic glue holding the novel together. (An exasperated Ali wonders '[h]ow many walls can one nation erect and sustain ...?' (51).) The fragility of love in the face of larger forces is made abundantly clear. At the time of its 2002 publication, *Kartography* was the most ambitious Shamsie novel to date. Yet it sometimes labours in its attempts to construct and maintain the parallels that give it shape. Some readers may find what the text calls its '[r]epeating patterns' (250) too obtrusive: the mixed-up lovers theme is cemented by references to *A Midsummer Night's Dream*, while the delayed elaboration of Raheen and Karim's shared family secret and the convoluted plotting feel overly schematic when compared to the deceptively clear, clean narrative lines of later novels such as *Home Fire*. Nonetheless, *Kartography* marks an important step in Shamsie's move away from a regional and family focus and towards an understanding of the inescapable influence of geography as well as history. Later books project this theme onto a global screen with a broader social canvas. Shamsie's next novel, *Broken Verses*, however, continues her investigation into the collision between despotism and the desires of the individual amidst the turmoil of Pakistani politics, considering once more how the past casts a shadow over the present.

*

In *Broken Verses* (2005), the two moments of the 1980s and the post-millennial era of Pakistan's involvement in the US-led global War on Terror are brought together in the story of Aasmaani, a young woman obsessed by the fate of her mother, Samina, who was a leading light of the 1980s women's movement protesting against General Zia ul-Haq's Islamisation campaign. The draconian changes wrought by the Zia government, through which it sought to implement an agenda favourable to the increasingly powerful right-wing religious forces in the country by governing Pakistan according to the principles of Shariah law, had particularly negative effects for women's rights. The drive to impose more conservative forms of dress on women, reduce their public visibility, and curtail their participation in politics led to a reversal of the gains they had made over the previous decades. Foremost among the attacks on women were the infamous Hudood Ordinances (1979) and the 1984 *Qanun-e-Shahadat* (Law of Evidence), oppressive reforms downgrading women's legal status by giving their testimonies a lower status than those of men and effectively sanctioning sexual violence against them.[8]

In *Offence*, Shamsie outlines some of the characteristics of the brand of Islam Zia sought to enforce: 'Lashing, amputation, stoning to death – all in public. Most offensive of all to Muslims for whom theirs was a religion of justice, the Hudood Ordinances allowed for rape victims to be tried for adultery and stoned to death'. The latter injunction was brought to global attention when, in 1983, 'Safia Bibi, a blind 13-year-old girl who was raped but couldn't identify her attackers, was found guilty of adultery and sentenced to imprisonment, a fine and a public lashing' while her attackers walked free.[9] Although the judgement in the Bibi case was eventually overturned, the increasing frequency of such miscarriages of justice in the early 1980s led to the formation of the Women's Action Forum, a feminist group set up to allow women to organise and fight back against the erosion of their rights. In the novel, Samina becomes a high-profile leader of the resulting protests, helping to arrange rallies and marches and becoming one of the movement's most articulate voices. She is frequently detained by the police and experiences their brutal tactics at first hand; Aasmaani remembers her mother returning from one rally 'with vicious bruises on her back and arms and stomach' (*Broken Verses*, 95).

For much of the 1980s, General Zia's authority was underpinned by support from the United States, which saw his regime as a key strategic ally in the fight against the Soviet occupation of Afghanistan.[10] In one of several ironic parallels between the two eras, the same Western powers that shored up Zia's religiously conservative military dictatorship in its fight against the Soviets are now, in Aasmaani's post-9/11 moment, demanding Pakistan's acquiescence in their own invasion of Afghanistan to root out Islamist terrorists. The West had also encouraged the opening up of Pakistan's notoriously tightly controlled media, in furtherance of those neoliberal economic policies pursued by Nawaz Sharif's government in the 1990s at the behest of the International Monetary Fund. These policies involved the sale of public assets and the shrinking of state provision in favour of aggressive economic privatisation.

Further events at the turn of the millennium also prompted the overhaul of broadcasting. Pakistan's arrival in the club of nations with nuclear capabilities in 1998 and the brief conflict between Pakistani and Indian forces in the Kargil district of Jammu and Kashmir the following year coincided with Pakistanis turning away from the state television channel, PTV, which had come to seem like a staid purveyor of ideology, and towards the entertainment provided by the new satellite channels mainly transmitting from India. The potential consequences of the drip-feed of messaging from the neighbouring enemy prompted action to create a more dynamic national mediascape. A liberalisation of the Pakistani media took place under General Pervaiz Musharraf, who had assumed the presidency in yet another military coup in 1999. Pursuing a policy of what was known as 'Enlightened Moderation', Musharraf portrayed his government as breaking with the political Islam of the Zia era, both in his cooperation with the Americans in the War on Terror and in the deregulation of the media. A reduction in the costs and red tape around setting up new television channels resulted in their proliferation in the early years of the twenty-first century. At the same time, television sets were becoming cheaper, resulting in a vast new viewership and untapped markets. Taha Kazi records that by 2006 there were over a hundred new channels 'vying for greater market share and advertising revenue'.[11] A further consequence was the relaxing of direct ideological control of media output in favour of an unofficial reciprocity whereby the government would tolerate a degree of independence from broadcasters as a way of securing its own reputation as a liberal force. Kazi cites Tahir Naqvi's view that 'the entry of several new players into the broadcasting industry created unprecedented opportunities for the production and circulation of unofficial meanings'.[12] Aasmaani celebrates the new opportunities for women to contribute to these meanings the first time she visits the studios of the production company for whom she will work. Noting the smart young women in executive positions, she remarks:

> They had that light in their eyes, those girls did, of believing they were a part of something bigger than their own lives. They

were going to beam youth culture, progressive thought, multiple perspectives, in-depth reporting to a nation that until so recently had only known news channels which spoke with the voice of the government. 2002 would be remembered as the year of the cable TV explosion in Pakistan, and these girls were right bang in the middle of it, making history happen. (4–5)

Soon after she begins her new job, old memories and unresolved anxieties are stirred for Aasmaani when she begins to receive from an anonymous source what appear to be newly penned love letters to her mother by her long-term paramour, Nazim, also known as Omi and often referred to by Aasmaani simply as 'the Poet'. Samina has left her marriage to Aasmaani's father to be with the charismatic scribe, and their tangled and ultimately doomed romance captivates all those with whom they come into contact. Omi's political trajectory recalls that of the real-world dissident writer Faiz Ahmed Faiz, whom Ali Madeeh Hashmi has described as 'Pakistan's most famous poet ... the man who had been a thorn in every Pakistani government's side since the country's formation in 1947'.[13] Like Faiz, Omi undergoes periods of imprisonment and self-imposed exile, is persecuted for his communist sympathies, and pens fierce yet lyrical poems against the injustices perpetrated by the government.[14] However, unlike Faiz, who was able to return to Pakistan and live out his days after years in exile, Omi has been tortured and murdered by unknown assailants and his unrecognisable body dumped, leading Samina to depression and an apparent suicide by drowning. Yet the letters, written in a code known only to the lovers, hold out the hope that Omi may in fact still be alive, held captive somewhere. The novel becomes a study in obsession as Aasmaani vacillates between belief and doubt regarding the letters' authenticity, always nurturing a forlorn hope that this irresistible figure from her childhood lives on somewhere. If Omi is still alive, perhaps Samina is too? The possibility brings increased emotional proximity to her mother, coupled with distress and disbelief in the circumstances of her apparent death. Aasmaani shares her mother's uncompromising determination, albeit leavened with a greater degree of cynicism manifest in a sardonic persona constructed for emotional self-protection. Aasmaani is another of Shamsie's guarded heroines, like Raheen in *Kartography*, who resist the vulnerability that comes with allowing others to get close. She finds herself stuck: unable to accept that her mother and the Poet are dead but lacking the forward-looking political commitments that gave their lives purpose.

In the course of charting Aasmaani's mental anguish, *Broken Verses* explores questions of character and identity: how much is inherited – her physical resemblance to her mother is often remarked upon – and how far the idea of character is invented to make sense of the endless ambiguity of motive animating any individual. Throughout the novel, Aasmaani struggles to understand the contradiction whereby her mother can, in a paroxysm of grief, leave all she has known, her political commitments and even her family, and choose suicide. Reflecting on the larger-than-life woman who was at once her mother *and* an inspiring beacon of the women's movement, Aasmaani asks:

> What connected the woman in all those images – the activist, the mother, the lover, the mourner, the dancer, the deserter? What allowed a single 'version' to arise from such variedness? There was a word for it: character. That imaginary tyrant. We pretend we all have one, and that it is something to be relied upon, something knowable and true, even when it oppresses and constrains us. When someone behaves 'out of character' we frown a little, a voice inside us whispering something that makes us uneasy, but then our brows clear. We've found a way to interpret the action as being in character. Or we say we were wrong about the person's character to begin with ... We don't dare to consider that the internal voice which makes us uneasy is a voice that whispers: there is no such thing as fixed character, there is only our need to join the dots into a single picture. (141–142)

Aasmaani acknowledges the danger of becoming a slave to notions of one's own character. Yet her recognition of the fictive nature of character – that its supposed development is actually 'the development of a storyline' (142) – fails to furnish her with sufficient scepticism when it comes to her mother and the Poet, leaving her susceptible to the wiles of the letter writer.

The notion of masks and the performance of different versions of the self finds its correlative in themes of drama and acting. Aasmaani is involved in television drama production and befriends Shehnaz Saeed, a veteran television star who suddenly retired at the height of her fame but who is now making a comeback by appearing in a soap opera, *Boond*.[15] Shehnaz is to play the emotionally evocative role of a long-absent mother who unexpectedly returns to her family. Life and art become entwined as Aasmaani learns more about the friendship between Shehnaz and her mother. She discovers that the actress harboured an unrequited love for Samina. Shehnaz is the precursor of Shamsie's first openly lesbian character, Maryam Khan in *Best of Friends*, and her complex sexuality aligns with Samina's disavowal of the hallowed role of domesticated Pakistani mother which sees her frequently abandon Aasmaani for periods of time to pursue her activism and to follow Omi on his travels. Samina rejects as false the 'choice to be made between motherhood and standing up for justice' (90). The life-choices of Samina and Shehnaz work, as Ruvani Ranasinha puts it, to 'contest fixed predetermined female subjectivities'. In her insistence on not being 'one of those women the beards approve of, the ones who sit at home and cook dinner' (59), Shehnaz 'successfully articulates the radical displacement of gender and sexual norms, whilst also reinforcing a secular feminist critique of patriarchal interpretations of Islam'.[16] In a touching scene during which Shehnaz comes closest to expressing her true feelings, stumbling through a 'tortured monologue' about identity and desire, Samina expresses her inclusive credo via an analogy: '"I've never liked mangoes. People say it means I'm not a true Pakistani, but I've never liked mangoes. Nothing to be done about it, and frankly I don't see why I should bother to try. The way I see it I'm just expanding people's notions of what it means to be Pakistani"' (297). We can read this whole exchange, and the attempt to express by other means what is unspeakable in a censorious society, as what Cara Cilano calls 'a challenge to essentialist categories' showing 'new ways to claim belonging within the family and within the nation'.[17]

In *Broken Verses* characters all possess secrets. The secret coded letters, deciphered by Aasmaani, appear to show that Omi is still alive and reveal more about his intimate life with Samina. Having grown up in a country fixated with political conspiracy theories, Aasmaani understands that the letters may be a hoax and determines to try to trace their provenance and if possible rescue Omi, all the while aware that by so doing she may attract the attention of the shadowy forces responsible for his disappearance.[18] Perspective and the desire to believe are all-important but can result in self-deception.

In the same way, language can be used either to expose lies or to conceal the truth. In contrast to the playful punning one finds in Shamsie's first three novels, here the irreverent use of language has consequences, as Omi finds out to his cost. The poetic and political potential of Urdu language and literature is a recurring source of inspiration as well as a motif for Shamsie. She has noted, for example, the key role feminist Urdu poets such as Fehmida Riaz played in articulating resistance to General Zia's regime.[19] Here, the power of language is inscribed through the snatches of verse we read and which are recollected by Aasmaani as she remembers the larger-than-life poet who courted her mother. Omi's Sufi-inspired aesthetic stands against the more severe Deobandi strain of Sunni Islam in the ascendant in 1980s Pakistan.[20] In his verse he exalts the love he shares with Samina, recasting them in his poetry as the legendary doomed lovers Layla and Majnun from the epic poem by the twelfth-century Persian poet Nizami, whose story he rewrites. In true Sufi style, Omi's masterpiece, *Laila*, describes the desire for oneness between lover and beloved. Yet the moment of consummation is also one of bitter disillusionment as Laila realises that oneness with the beloved means complete self-effacement (49). There is also a tension between Omi's imaginative longings and Samina's practical activism, with the challenge to reconcile them never quite being met. (We hear of a parallel instance of Samina's effective use of language when Aasmaani discovers an old recording of her mother going head-to-head with a conservative cleric in a public debate at the height of General Zia's repression in 1986. Although her impassioned rhetoric gets the better of the sarcastic, stolid cleric, its declarative certainty is not enough to prevent her succumbing to despair after Omi's death.) The difficulty, for Aasmaani, in seeing her complex mother clearly is emphasised when her cuckolded father cuts through the mythologisation the couple have undergone to recall Samina as 'entirely human, entirely breakable, and entirely extraordinary' (332).

Obsession and melancholia have allowed the past to haunt the present, preventing Aasmaani from moving on. In the end, we discover that the supposedly authentic letters have been forged by Shehnaz's son Adnan (known as Ed), a returnee from the United States who also works for the television station and begins a tentative flirtation with Aasmaani. He hopes to use the letters to pierce the carapace of her cynical persona and reach the woman beneath. His deception ends their budding romance and brings Aasmaani to the point of a nervous breakdown. Yet, inadvertently it also becomes the means by which she starts to come to terms with her mother's and the Poet's deaths. To move on she needs to find in herself the same kind of strength that allowed Samina to confront and best the conservative Islamic cleric all those years earlier. The closing scene sees her pitching a documentary about the 1980s women's movement to a rival channel in time for the twentieth anniversary of the Hudood Ordinances, a move guaranteed to rile those religious parties who still hold sway in many parts of Pakistan.

At the end, Aasmaani makes peace with the permanent loss of her mother and the Poet, moving in Freudian terms from melancholia to genuine mourning.[21] The novel concludes with a private ritual of farewell on a Karachi beach in which Aasmaani consigns her mother's name, written in sand, to the waves. This marks the final appearance of that water imagery which wends its way through the novel, beginning with the opening dream of an elusive mermaid, but this time implying a cleansing release from the burdens of the past and a turning to the future. In Shamsie's fiction, heroic women such as Samina are often associated with martyrdom. Yet their sacrifices open a space for the questioning of prevailing orthodoxies, thereby allowing for the possibility of change in the next generation.

4.

The Webs of History: *Burnt Shadows* and *A God in Every Stone*

When Samina confronts the conservative Islamic cleric in the recorded debate which Aasmaani discovers near the end of *Broken Verses*, she challenges him not only on his repressive and partisan interpretation of the Quran's teachings about female modesty, but also about the long-term cost of the anti-Soviet *jihad* in Afghanistan which the clerisy supports. She berates him for sending 'those young, idealistic ... ready-to-be brainwashed boys' off to fight, and asks, 'What happens after Afghanistan, have you considered that? Where do they go next, those global guerrillas with their allegiance to a common cause and their belief in violence as the most effective way to take on the enemy? Do you and your American friends ever sit down to talk about that?' (*Broken Verses*, 285, 286). Shamsie's next novel, *Burnt Shadows* (2009), offers a substantial answer to Samina's urgent question, tracing the blowback experienced when these Islamist militants turned their ire on the Western sponsors who had abandoned them but, at the same time, linking the contemporary conflict to the residue of that imperialism and nationalism which blighted the twentieth century.

In its concern for the consequences of Western interference in South Asia, *Burnt Shadows* pursues Shamsie's interest in the legacies of the past outward from Pakistan and onto the global stage. The novel takes us from the dropping of the atomic bomb on Nagasaki at the end of World War Two to the years after 9/11 with their mix of ethnic and religious discrimination, via what for Shamsie is the linchpin decade of the 1980s, where

American post-imperial meddling played a direct role in the rise of Islamist terrorism. The story of two interconnected family units, the Tanaka-Ashrafs and the Weiss-Burtons, is not only international but also trans-temporal: their fates entwined with the story of the twentieth century itself. To better encompass the enlarged canvas here, Shamsie refines her narrative technique. As Claire Chambers has noted, in *Burnt Shadows* 'she eschews the first-person narrator used in her previous three novels in favour of free indirect discourse and multiple perspectives, widening her scope from upper-class Karachi to encompass Japan, India, Afghanistan and America as well as Pakistan'. Commenting on this shift, Shamsie offers an insight into the priorities and resulting narrative strategies that have come increasingly to shape her fiction: '[t]he characters come first for me: I want to explore how history impacts on their lives, rather than using them as a vehicle to talk about history. I wrote in free indirect discourse because this time I wanted to create a tapestry, rather than a novel with one central character like my others'.[1]

Hiroko Tanaka is a *hibakusha*, a survivor of the United States' attack on Nagasaki on 9 August 1945. The bomb shatters her world literally, as she picks her way through the devastation of her home city, and emotionally, since the bomb has taken the life of her lover, a German émigré named Konrad Weiss. Their blossoming romance symbolises the syncretic potential of a Japanese city where multicultural influences are present even in the architecture. Yet their love has developed also in the shadow of war and its attendant nationalist prejudices. Like all close relationships in this novel, it is fragile and easily snuffed out.[2]

Hiroko uproots herself after the war and travels to Delhi, bearing the stigmata of the crane-shaped shadows seared onto her skin by the atomic blast. She arrives at the home of Konrad's sister Ilse, also known as Elizabeth, and her English husband, James Burton, just at the moment when the British are about to leave India in 1947. Here she meets Sajjad Ashraf, a promising young Indian with ambitions for a career in law whom James has taken under his wing. Hiroko and Sajjad tentatively begin a cross-racial courtship which is at first misunderstood by the Europeans, with their strict anti-miscegenation prejudices. Hiroko and Elizabeth at the same time find fellowship in their shared sense of suffocation at the hands of patriarchal nationalism. The Indian section ends with Elizabeth and James estranged and about to leave India to re-join their young son Harry back in England, and Sajjad about to lose his beloved 'Dilli' – the multiplicitous native part of the city he holds dear – to the bitter divisions of Partition.

As these and subsequent sections show, the novel is shaped by some of the major upheavals of the twentieth century. Characters are caught up in global tribulations and all experience the loss of loved ones and beloved homes. They become peripatetic, settling for a few years in one place before being forced by circumstances and politics to move on again. In the next generation, Harry, to whom England is only ever a 'way station' (*Burnt Shadows*, 169), finds his own youthful idealism better reflected in the United States' inclusivity, becoming a citizen and rising to a senior rank in the security service. Yet even he is ultimately vulnerable. As his storyline approaches its tragic conclusion we are reminded of this shared precarity: 'Hiroko, Sajjad, Konrad, Ilse, Harry: history had blown all of them off course, no one ending ... where they had begun' (282).

The pattern of repetition in a century disfigured by hostile ethnic and religious nationalism gives the novel a thematic and formal coherence. It is prefigured by a brief prologue where we are introduced to an as-yet-unnamed figure in shackles being stripped in a detention facility. '*How did it come to this,* he wonders' (1), and the story thereafter explains. The opening context is the immediate aftermath of 9/11, the detainee is Hiroko and Sajjad's son Raza, and his likely destination is the US detention camp at Guantanamo Bay in Cuba, used to hold terror suspects. A gifted linguist, Raza has become a freelance operative in Afghanistan during the so-called War on Terror years at the beginning of the twenty-first century. Falsely accused of involvement in the murder of his uncle Harry, Raza finds himself on the run, eventually trading places with an illegal immigrant to the US to whom he feels indebted, before being captured by law-enforcement officers. The implied symbolic link between the Nagasaki bomb and the 9/11 attacks is less to do with any simple historical or moral equivalence and more with the way such atrocities force people apart, entrench hatred, and ensure the cycle of violence will continue into the future.

Indeed, the novel has a persistent concern with what humans will do to one another, given conducive circumstances. Hiroko experiences the full horror of this at Nagasaki and it makes her a principled anti-nationalist, opposed to the unreasoning zeal required to stoke conflict. She is dismayed equally by the unwavering fidelity to the Japanese emperor that sends young kamikaze pilots hurtling to their deaths in World War Two; religious nationalism in the Islamic Republic of Pakistan, stoked by America as an aid to unseating the Russians from their occupation of neighbouring Afghanistan in the 1980s; and the blind patriotism required even in cosmopolitan New York after the 9/11 attacks. *Burnt Shadows* maintains a sensitive distinction between the 'human', the 'inhuman' (as an adjective to describe types of atrocity), and 'unhuman', signifying the mental and corporeal dehumanisation of victims in acts such as those which took place at Hiroshima and Nagasaki. Hiroko is haunted by the memory of seeing her father, charred and reptilian, crawling half-dead towards her moments after the attack: 'I thought he was something unhuman' (99). Summing up what she has learned, she recalls: 'When Konrad first heard of the concentration camps he said you have to deny people their humanity in order to decimate them. You don't ... You just have to put them in a little corner of the big picture' (362). Part of the novel's strength is in imputing responsibility for, rather than abstracting, apocalyptic violence. Atrocities are always a result of willed acts conducted by parties bent on their own strategic goals, regardless of the cost to others.

Among the crisis points in global post-war history, the connected moments of America's arming of *mujahideen* militants fighting the Soviet occupation of Afghanistan and the 9/11 attacks come to dominate the second half of *Burnt Shadows*. The *mujahideen* was a militia force supported financially and militarily by the United States in what was codenamed 'Operation Cyclone', part of the last phase of the Cold War before the Soviet Union collapsed at the end of the 1980s. The regional effect of this action is a topic Shamsie's fiction frequently revisits. As she notes in *Offence: The Muslim Case* quoting Eqbal Ahmed, '[t]he Afghan War brought "the Kalashnikov culture" to Pakistan as the country became "the world's largest open market in arms". From here on, anyone with a grudge to settle or a point to make would have a weapon'.[3]

In the novel, the ripples of the Afghan campaign spread into the 1990s, when the withdrawal of the Soviet empire led first to civil war in Afghanistan and then to the ascent to power of the Taliban regime and its various hangers-on. Among them was the kernel of what would become Al Qaeda, established in 1988 by Osama Bin Laden, a member of a wealthy Saudi family. Following his expulsion from Saudi Arabia for speaking out against the regime's alliance with the United States, Bin Laden eventually took refuge in Afghanistan, where he built up Al Qaeda, conducting terrorist attacks on US interests around the world, culminating in the 9/11 attacks in 2001.[4]

In the novel's 1980s section, Raza, disaffected and failing at school, befriends Abdullah, a young gun-runner for the *mujahideen* who regularly journeys to Peshawar and the militia camps beyond the border. He joins Abdullah on one such expedition, passing himself off as 'Raza Hazara' in a daring act which indirectly results in the death of his father, Sajjad, who has set out to find him, but which also draws the attention of Harry Burton, now a senior US intelligence operative. Harry is intrigued by the boy's ability to pass unsuspected in the hinterlands of Afghanistan, much like Rudyard Kipling's imperial boy spy Kim in the novel of that name (1901). Twenty years later they both find themselves working for an American private security firm in the country, post-9/11. Afghanistan is now a space of war, but also of capitalist opportunism.[5]

At its moral centre, *Burnt Shadows* valorises those characters who seek connections, between the past and the present, and between themselves and others. Hiroko is the most obvious example. Her life's experiences have taught her the value in seeing connecting threads, but also in resisting the kind of facile historical conflations particularly popular in the War on Terror years. The attack on New York in 2001 was read in some quarters as a replaying of Pearl Harbor, and the subsequent one-sided yet diffuse conflict as a heroic rebooting of a 'just war' for our times. Writing of the same moment, Mohsin Hamid's protagonist in *The Reluctant Fundamentalist* notes the 'dangerous nostalgia' overtaking the US: 'There was something undeniably retro about the flags and the uniforms, about generals addressing cameras in war rooms and newspaper headlines featuring words such as *duty* and *honor*'.[6] For her part, Hiroko – who has found a spiritual home in multicultural New York – is moved by the plight of those left bereaved and desperate after 9/11 yet, having suffered the effects of America's own atomic atrocity fifty-five years earlier, she is unpersuaded by the accompanying rhetoric of exceptionalism. Madeline Clements describes the 'scrupulously unaffiliated' position Hiroko cultivates that allows her 'to engage with planetary others whose nominal regional, cultural and religious allegiances make them vulnerable to xenophobic attacks'.[7] While gazing at posters of the missing in New York, she observes that, 'In times such as these it seemed entirely wrong to feel oneself living in a different history to the people of this city' (274).

A central metaphor for the ties that bind is that of a web. Taking its inspiration from the story of the spider whose web is said to have protected the Prophet Muhammad while he was sheltering from pursuers in a cave, the web image comes to have multiple meanings in the novel, linking temporal and spatial experience. On a return visit to those parts of colonial India where he grew up, Harry Burton feels 'the gnarly stuff of space and time which separated him from his childhood thin to cobwebs' (148); and the Weiss-Burton and Tanaka-Ashraf families are described as 'each other's spiders' (350) woven together by loyalty and affection. Harry muses: 'Whatever might be happening in the wider world, at least the Weiss-Burtons and the Tanaka-Ashrafs had finally found spaces to cohabit in, complicated shared history giving nothing but depth to the reservoir of their friendships' (277). Yet, precisely because they are multiracial units in a century of nationalist belligerence, the diversity they embody is constantly under threat. As the novel reaches its climax we discover that webs can have a much stickier, ensnaring effect if spun so as to entrap others. Harry's daughter Kim, a New Yorker traumatised by the 9/11 attacks and her father's death, comes to embody a worldview now less open to difference and more inclined to treat others – especially Muslim others – as a threat. She unwittingly becomes the means by which Raza is captured when she reports on Abdullah, now an illegal immigrant in America, who she is supposed to be taking to a rendezvous with a rescuer. She begins to have doubts about Abdullah's innocence when, in her raw emotional state, she perceives a veiled threat in his observation that the US tends to fight its wars 'somewhere else': 'It's why you fight more wars than anyone else; because you understand war least of all. You need to understand it better' (344). When she drops him off at the appointed location, she notifies the police, leading to Raza's arrest in a case of mistaken identity, an error Kim finds she has no power to rectify.

Burnt Shadows exemplifies Shamsie's increasing range, expanding from an almost exclusive focus on the lives of the South Asian elite to encompass a much broader social spectrum. Its cast of characters are all on the move. The more fortunate ones can choose their homeland while those who find themselves in the wrong place at the wrong time are forcibly uprooted by the political turmoil of the twentieth century. Cara Cilano has argued that this and other post-9/11 novels by Pakistani writers 'can promote collective identifications, moving the idea of the nation away from traditional notions of consanguinity and soil' and envisaging other modes of solidarity.[8] Ever adaptable and on the move, humans can identify with new homes as well as with old. According to Cilano, as a Partition migrant, 'Sajjad Ashraf ... becomes Pakistani against his convictions ... [his] *mohajir* identity ensconces him rather securely in one of Pakistan's most powerful founding myths',[9] while Ahmed Gamal argues that the novel 'fundamentally problematizes the condition of migrancy by deconstructing the binarism of home and the world'.[10] At its heart, however, *Burnt Shadows* is a book about the forced migrations of the second half of the twentieth century and beyond, those that indicate the limits of the nation state's inclusivity and point up the perils of statelessness. To peregrinating victims of mid-century upheavals, such as Hiroko and Sajjad, we can add the hundreds of thousands of refugees set on the move by tectonic shifts in geopolitics caused by the War on Terror. Abdullah represents this class most directly, but Raza also gains a taste of its extreme experiences when, divested of all identifying documentation, he attempts to escape from the American forces who wrongly suspect him of complicity in Harry's murder. His flight involves being crammed in with dozens of other refugees beneath the false deck of a small motorboat undertaking the ocean crossing – an experience which reminds him of news footage of the mass graves in Kosovo but which might also resonate with the reader as an echo of the fate of African slaves in the Middle Passage. The 'Wretched of the Earth' are always with us. Once more the 'unhuman' status of such human cargo is to the fore – symbolised by the bizarre last leg of Raza's journey back to North America, which he is forced to undertake inside a gorilla suit in a cargo plane full of exotic animals. Such direct contemporary political concerns give *Burnt Shadows* a more capacious feel than previous novels. I have elsewhere proposed that we read it as a 'global' novel, describing 'subjects and situations that are the result of the logic of globalisation, at the same time thereby ... awakening in the reader a new awareness of the costs of that process'.[11]

The title of the final section, 'The Speed Necessary to Replace Loss', is taken from Michael Ondaatje's 1992 Booker Prize-winning novel, *The English Patient*.[12] *Burnt Shadows* shares with that earlier novel an interest in the coming together of diverse characters in conditions of war and the links which are tentatively, fitfully nurtured in the face of atrocities committed in the name of nations. There is a similar attention to the impact of the converging histories protagonists always carry with them and which are in tension with their desire to reach out to each other.[13] Shamsie's novel insistently asks such questions as: what of these fledgling relationships can be retained? And what kind of literary language can make audible the uniqueness of historically grounded experience amid the din made by the ignorant armies of blinkered patriotism? We might say, then, that Shamsie's project is similar to that which animated the work of E. M. Forster a century earlier: the need to 'only connect'. Indeed, there are marked echoes of, and allusions to, Forster's most famous work, *A Passage to India* (1924), in the Delhi section of *Burnt Shadows*: Sajjad is first seen cycling through the streets of Delhi to the Burton's property in the Civil Lines district, musing on his ancestors and the British, much as Dr Aziz does in Forster's novel (33); the physical manifestation of his increasing closeness to Hiroko is at first misinterpreted as an attempted sexual assault (92), after which he declares himself 'done with the English' (105); it is evident that his close friendship with James Burton will – like that of Aziz and Fielding – not survive Partition; and there are even direct references to *A Passage to India* at one point, when James expresses his disappointment at its 'disgrace of an ending' (111).[14]

In the strong intertextual invocation of Forster in the Delhi section of *Burnt Shadows*, so insistent as to momentarily interrupt the novel's dominant realism, Shamsie takes perhaps the first step on a path towards a fully worked out recognition that coming to terms with the legacies of colonial history in particular requires engaging with some of the still-living myths and stereotypes that cultural and literary representations have enshrined. This will eventually lead to *Home Fire*'s wholesale interrogation and partial rejection of realism as the default means by which to make sense of, and render for a reader, the disconnected experiences of lives torn apart by revenant imperial ways of thinking in the modern world. A blend of realistic detail, melodrama, and myth comes together to form what we might call a mythic realism in Shamsie's later work, as tonal shifts and epic scenarios intrude on the mundane yet oppressive operations of politics that work to silence those whose opposition to colonial and neo-colonial power is not recognised in official discourse.

*

A concern to trace back in time the workings of empire animates a more directly historical novel, *A God in Every Stone* (2014). This text is perhaps Shamsie's most concerted attempt to date at integrating two of her main recurring preoccupations, geography and history. They are embodied in the theme of archaeology and the degree to which a version of the past of a place is retrievable in the present. Such retrieval is always inherently imaginative, requiring the art of storytelling to connect up and make audible the echoes of other times. History and geography come together in the archaeological interests that unite an independent Englishwoman called Vivian Spencer and a young Peshawari boy, Najeeb Gul, who meet during the inter-war years of the early twentieth century. They are brought together in a quest for an ornamental gold crown, said to have been discovered in the fifth century BC by a Carian general, Scylax, and now believed to be buried somewhere near Peshawar. The crown (or 'circlet') provides the ostensible object of desire, but the story is more centrally about the final days of the British Empire and what happens to those Indians who have served it.

This is another of Shamsie's novels to deploy what we might term multiple time signatures; the book begins with a fragment from the fifth century BC, telling the story of Scylax's arrival in Caspatyrus – a name taken to refer to the site of modern-day Peshawar – in the service of Darius's Persian Empire. Scylax finds there the crown, or 'circlet', the present location of which becomes the primary focus of a search by characters in the early twentieth century. Yet, as Herodotus records, within a few years Scylax was fighting on behalf of his own Carian people *against* Darius's imperial forces, and this turn against empire forms another thematic strand, with the bulk of the novel set during the crucial years of the Indian independence struggle from World War One to the beginning of the 1930s.

Two characters embody opposition to the still-oppressive empires of the early twentieth century: Tahsin Bey, a charismatic Turkish archaeologist and the intended husband of the novel's female historian protagonist, Vivian, whose Armenian sympathies lead to his assassination by Ottoman agents during the Great War; and Qayyum, a Peshawari Pathan who finds himself on the battlefields of the Western Front, serving a British Empire which discriminates against the Indian troops it has conscripted to fight for it. Initially an anglophile, Qayyum becomes disenchanted when, after losing an eye at Ypres, he discovers that his battlefield rescuer and fellow Peshawari, Kalam Khan, has been imprisoned for attempted desertion. Khan recognises the paradox of Muslim soldiers fighting for their imperial overlords, often against their fellow Muslim Turks. On his return to Peshawar, Qayyum joins the real-life freedom fighter Ghaffar Khan, fabled reformer and apostle of non-violence, to focus on raising education levels and campaigning against the British.[15]

Occupying a more ambivalent space is Qayyum's younger brother, Najeeb. We first meet him as a boy, guiding Vivian around Peshawar on her arrival. He is soon taken under her wing and, inspired by her lessons in the history and mythology of the region, goes to college, eventually obtaining a post as Indian Assistant at the Peshawar museum where he previously spent many happy hours. At the adult Najeeb's prompting, Vivian is lured back to Peshawar years later by the promise of an archaeological dig aimed at discovering the location of Scylax's circlet. Najeeb is also a consummate storyteller, dubbed by Vivian the 'Herodotus of Peshawar'. He crafts tales imagining the ancient adventures of Scylax which are transformed into ballads by those who ply their trade on the Street of Storytellers. For Najeeb, history and imagination are inextricably linked in a lineage of stories connected by place. He is inspired by 'all these stories which happened where we live, on our piece of earth – how can you stay immune to them?' (*A God in Every Stone*, 181).

As an intercessor between the increasingly opposed cultures of Europe and Asia, Najeeb at first embodies potential connections; at the museum he consciously pairs two sculpted heads 'of almost identical size, one Greek in features, one Indian, separated by three centuries or more' (239). We learn that 'what he loves most about Peshawar is the proximity of the past. All around the broken bowl of the Peshawar valley his glance knows how to burn away time. So, in a single day he might encounter the Chinese monk Fa Hien throwing flowers into the Buddha's alms bowl; ... the Khushan King Kanushka; ... the Mughal Emperor Babur; ... the Sikh Maharajah Ranjit Singh' (272). The novel describes such historical and mythological palimpsests as moments when 'time braids': 'There goes Babur's spear, missing a rhino and wounding Nearchus who falls at the feet of a Ghandaran sculptor carving a stupa with Atlas at its base holding up the elevated figure of the Buddha which Marco Polo sketches on a leaf stolen out of his hand by Scylax and buried deep in the ground by an unnamed heroine to protect it from the marauding White Huns' (272). Remnants of pre-Islamic culture lie everywhere.[16] Commenting on the debilitating effect of censorship and narrow religious outlooks, Shamsie has said: 'to a large extent we Pakistanis don't fully understand what our history is ... If you don't understand contemporary history, how can you know your earlier history? We should be saying that anything that happened in the geographical territory is Pakistan's history, including the rich Buddhist and Hindu pasts from Taxila, Harappa, and the Indus Valley civilization, but post-Partition rhetoric about Muslimness and Islam makes this hard to do'.[17] Equally enthused by the multiple sedimented legacies she uncovers in her archaeological work, Vivian describes this mix as 'syncretic' (86).[18]

Yet the enjoyment of place and the past is neither unalloyed nor immune from power dynamics. The now-activist Qayyum berates his brother for what he sees as an apolitical relativism which serves the values of the coloniser: 'Your museums are all part of their Civilising Mission, their White Man's Burden, the moral justification for what they have done here' (185). In a colonial context the question of the power to classify and organise knowledge is as pressing as that of who owns the land itself. Vivian is initially excited by the prospect of the British authorities launching a compulsory acquisition order against the intransigent landowner of the site she wishes to excavate. Nor is she above pulling imperial strings to get her way. Yet running parallel to the Westerner's desire to 'rescue' the past of another culture are longstanding traditions which such interventions blindly sweep away. Kalam's father tells Qayyum of the customary Pashtun system of land-sharing in which 'land was never owned but regularly redistributed between the tribes so no one could take control over the most fertile and everyone had sufficient wealth to live with honour'. This system has 'tottered on with more justice than most systems ... Until your English shredded it with their laws ... in order to create a class of landowners loyal to the crown' (140). Vivian's supposedly neutral historical interests merge with her coloniser's ability to possess and exploit land that belongs to others – a metaphor for the Raj's broader appropriations. The forcible control of land is repeatedly associated with death in the book – the excavation site sits next to a graveyard – while, as the climactic imperial massacre begins, Qayyum reflects: 'If a man is to die defending a land let the land be his land, the people his people' (205).

Despite being a comparatively open-minded representative of the imperial power, Vivian finds that her own journey of rebellion against an oppressive patriarchal culture in Britain can only bring her into a certain limited proximity to the India of which she has grown fond. She begins as an unconventional, well-educated, independently minded young Edwardian woman who has benefited from the additional, if limited, opportunities for women the war has thrown up. Reflecting on these changes as far as they affect her archaeological interests, Vivian notes: 'Today if a woman archaeologist were to suggest going to Cairo to work on maps no one would laugh. Gertrude Bell had joined

[T. E.] Lawrence at the Arab Bureau, and it was whispered that Margaret Hasluck was with Intelligence too' (264).[19] She has her parents' support, yet her father's favour seems more a way of compensating for his lack of a son than suggesting any great faith in Vivian's abilities. His expectations of patriotic self-sacrifice are transferred onto his daughter who finds herself obediently nursing wounded troops in Brighton. More disastrously, she is pressurised into revealing Tahsin Bey's political sympathies to a British intelligence officer, as a result of which he is murdered. It requires the intervention of her perspicacious mother – another of Shamsie's strong maternal characters – who understands Vivian's unspoken desires, before she can pursue her true ambition and travel to Peshawar in search of Scylax's circlet, following the trail Tahsin Bey has left for her.

As an intelligent young woman coming of age in the era of the suffragettes, much of Vivian's life seems to consist of defying male injunctions. In India she finds herself the object of stifling scrutiny by male members of the British community. The political agent, Remmick, who at one point seems a potential suitor, disapproves of her freely associating with Indians such as Najeeb. He believes this relationship and her previous closeness to Tahsin Bey reveal 'proclivities' (249) of a dangerously miscegenous kind. Initial contrasts are drawn between the self-sufficient Western woman and the largely faceless – literally so, given the preponderance of burqas in Peshawar – local women. Yet Vivian recognises that the same impulse to cover and thus control women is at work in the presence of the grille in the Ladies Gallery at the Palace of Westminster back in London, preventing the presence of women from distracting the male law-givers in the House of Commons below, which was only removed after suffragette campaigning in 1917. Although Vivian initially dismisses the burqa as oppressive, later she dons the garment to escape the scrutiny of the over-attentive Remmick. Moving unobserved across the city, she feels like 'just another local woman' (261), her sartorial 'betrayal' of the Raj allowing a new de-Orientalised view in which the power and violence needed to preserve empire is appreciated for the first time.

For all her rebelliousness, Vivian can never really be a part of this country standing on the verge of independence. As the book approaches its long, concluding set-piece scene – a depiction of the real-life 1930 Qissa Khwani massacre, when British troops attacked demonstrators from Gaffar Khan's *Khudai Khidmatgar* movement, resulting in many deaths – local women of the kind to whom she has previously condescended increasingly take centre stage. They are seen to be proactive in the independence struggle: from the prostitutes who offer safe haven to protesters being pursued by the British, to the sister-in-law pairing of Zarina and Diwa from the carpet-seller's family whose acts of charity and remembrance bring the novel to a close.[20] The mysterious, green-eyed Diwa in particular becomes a powerful warrior woman, at first giving water to the demonstrators penned in on the street beneath her bedroom balcony and thereafter – described in semi-mythological terms as an 'angel' or the Afghan folk hero Malalai of Maiwand reborn (281) – plunging from her balcony into the male crowd below: 'She pushes through the crowd. A man puts his hand on her shoulder to stop her ... and she roars at him, a sound which might have had words in it but she's not sure it does. His hands spring away from her as though she is a flame. She barrels through the crowd feeling herself on fire, no one must stop her, no one must even try' (290). In her transfiguration, Diwa anticipates Aneeka in *Home Fire*, who is similarly transformed into an epic figure, able to summon the elements to witness her grief. Our first introduction to Diwa comes when a passer-by relates how 'the angel' has been shot down by a British bullet. In other words, she is introduced as already a martyr. Characteristically, in Shamsie's novels, heroic women come to be associated with martyrdom: sometimes that of another but oftentimes their own, and they require a more exalted register to record their exploits. The everyday and the epic are fused in the sacrifice of extraordinary women.

A God in Every Stone is another novel centred on a quest. In Shamsie's work certain departed characters often serve as the initiators of the quests on which protagonists embark. They operate as those 'dispatchers' identified as crucial to the structure of tales in Vladimir Propp's celebrated narratological character schema.[21] The aunt in *Salt and Saffron*, the mother and the poet in *Broken Verses*, and the dead father in *Home Fire* all serve this function. Here, Tahsin Bey's cryptic final letter sets Vivian off on the hunt for the resting place of Scylax's circlet. In fact, in a somewhat unlikely turn of events, Najeeb finds the circlet, only to lose it again during the violent scenes that bring the book to a close. The circlet is less a tangible object that can be possessed than a symbol of questing itself. In the novel, the search for buried treasures gives way to the frantic quest for Najeeb when he temporarily goes missing during the violence, and Zarina's tragic and fruitless search for Diwa's body.

As in *Burnt Shadows*, so here the narrative once again leans heavily on intertextual borrowings from Raj fiction. Vivian has both the naivety of Forster's Adela Quested, determined to see 'the real India', and the sympathetic openness to difference of Mrs Moore. Here, as in *A Passage to India* and Paul Scott's *Raj Quartet*, colonial mandarins like Remmick see Indians as specifically threatening to English women, while his fellow club members mutter about murderous Pathans descending from the hills. Before first-hand experience of colonial violence disabuses her, Vivian enthuses about 'Kipling's Peshawar! The North West Frontier! ... It was immensely comforting to know oneself in a world in which battles followed the template laid down in books of adventure and valour. The words "Khyber Pass" sat on her tongue, fizzing with romance' (84). Such intertextual resonances are arguably more closely wedded to the novel's subject matter than in the somewhat more strained correspondences of *Burnt Shadows*. Yet, in both cases, we might see these moments as extensions of the mythic realist technique Shamsie has evolved: using myths from the South Asian and classical European traditions *and* interrogating those imperialist myths and stereotypes seen still to have a purchase on the contemporary imagination.

A God in Every Stone is a historical romance, albeit one containing darker meditations on the brutality of colonialism and the cost of opposing it. The novel's concern for authenticity is underpinned by the lengthy dramatisation of the Qissa Khwani massacre – one of the decisive moments in the independence struggle – as the narrative circles around the confusion to take in the different perspectives of the key protagonists. It is also there in a final 'End Note' which takes the form of an excerpt from the official report by Olaf Caroe, secretary to the Chief Commissioner, revealing the fate of those bodies that disappeared during the massacre. This short segment, drawn from the imperial archive itself, brings together the preceding fictional threads in which Zarina reburies the circlet in a ritual act of mourning and farewell that calls back to *Broken Verses'* final scene and also anticipates the denouement of *Home Fire*; Vivian accepts that the widening gulf between British and Indian means that her Forsterian desire to connect is doomed to failure; and Najeeb composes one last ballad imagining Scylax refusing to reveal the circlet's whereabouts to the emperor Darius's widow – a story that serves also as a statement of anticolonial defiance. Imperialist claims to both land and history are refuted once and for all.

As Shamsie's only historical novel to date, *A God in Every Stone* allows for a more direct reckoning with empire. An additional author's note on 'The inspiration behind *A God in Every Stone*' in a later paperback edition reveals that her original intention was to write a story about an archaeological search for Scylax's circlet set partly in 1930, drawing in Ghaffar Khan's movement and the Qissa Khwani massacre, and partly in the twenty-first century when the fundamentalist forces of the Taliban pose a threat to the syncretic vision of history the novel celebrates.[22] The final version dispenses with the contemporary moment to interrogate more directly the injustices that spurred on the independence struggle. Noting the novel's appearance around the centenary of the outbreak of World War One, Tara Talwar Windsor claims that *A God in Every Stone* 'addresses important blind spots in the literary and wider cultural memory of the war' – a cultural memory that has tended to be overwhelmingly Eurocentric. For Windsor, the novel presents 'a timely account of a range of hitherto hidden or marginalised histories, particularly in relation to the role of women and the experiences of South Asian soldiers, as well as colonial violence and anti-colonial resistance in the war's aftermath', which works to 'decentre and complicate traditional narratives', offering a more inclusive mode of commemorating this key moment in twentieth-century history.[23] In Shamsie's next novel, the postcolonial residue of the racialised power seen in action in *A God in Every Stone* falls on the marginalised citizens of contemporary, multicultural Britain.

5.

At Home in the World: *Home Fire* and *Best of Friends*

While writing *A God in Every Stone*, Shamsie was entering the final stages of her application process for British citizenship. Having initially entered the UK in 2007 on a Writers, Artists and Composers visa, her journey to citizenship coincided with a change of government, from Labour to the Conservative party, and a tightening up of the categories and requirements for migrants wishing to make the UK their home. In an essay entitled 'Everest is Climbed', she describes how the subsequent series of adjustments to immigration law, coupled with increasingly hostile rhetoric which began to separate '"the British" from "British passport-holders"', led to a sense of insecurity. Having gained indefinite leave to remain in 2012, Shamsie became a British citizen the following year but was greeted by a letter of welcome from the then home secretary, Theresa May, who had just launched an aggressive campaign against those migrants without the correct legal status – sending vans advising those who were in the UK illegally to 'go home' or face arrest. Shamsie recalls how, not long after, 'May called for powers to strip Britons of their citizenship in particular circumstances, if they were born outside the UK'.[1]

A sense of the perils of migrant status and the precarity of citizenship inform Shamsie's next two novels, beginning with *Home Fire* in 2017. In this, her most highly acclaimed novel so far, Shamsie retains the transnational focus characteristic of her later fiction, but also extends her range. *Home Fire* marks both a continuation of, and a departure from, the preoccupations and techniques of Shamsie's previous writing. While the novel is still concerned with family secrets and their fallout, the focus here is on the British Pakistani diaspora and its contrasting fates in the West after 9/11. There is also a wider social canvas, which allows for more detailed consideration of migrants beyond the cosmopolitan elite. Here the working-class Pasha siblings from an unfashionable area of North London share equal billing with the well-heeled family of the first Muslim to become British home secretary, Karamat Lone. Lone's story is itself another kind of migration narrative; he has grown up on streets like those where the Pashas now live but, through determination, hard work, and a strategic disavowal of his Muslim background, has moved up the social scale, carving out a successful political career with the party of government when the novel begins. Yet, far from being a celebration of hard graft and social mobility, *Home Fire* instead recognises those tightening constraints around Muslims in the West which were a feature of the years after the 11 September 2001 attacks on America and the 7 July 2005 assault on the London transport system, and which called into question their loyalty to Britain. For the Pashas, the ensuing suspicion is compounded by the loss of their father, who disappeared to pursue *jihad* in Bosnia in the 1990s and later died on the way to the Guantanamo Bay detention facility after 9/11. As events unfold, the legacy of his action and the governmental response to it, led by Lone, comes decisively to shape the family's fate.

Home Fire is a direct reworking of Sophocles' fifth-century-BC play *Antigone*, a canonical tragedy in which duty to the state collides with love of, and loyalty to, family. The play provides a framework within which characters and plot move. Sophocles' siblings Antigone, Polynices, and Ismene become Aneeka, Parvaiz, and Isma Pasha; Polynices' betrayal and attack on Thebes is echoed in Parvaiz's defection to the Islamic State militant group operating out of Syria; Creon, King of Thebes, becomes Karamat Lone, the home secretary who forbids the repatriation of Parvaiz's body after his death so as not to sully the soil he has betrayed; Creon's son Haemon, who is in love with Antigone, reappears in the form of the Home Secretary's son Ayman, who has changed his name to Eamonn in order, like his father, to distance himself from his Muslim heritage; while Aneeka, Antigone-like, enacts a ritual of mourning for the brother refused a burial in his homeland.[2] Inasmuch as Shamsie's story maps closely onto its ancient Greek inspiration, we might expect a certain schematism driving the plot to its inevitable conclusion. Yet the taut energy of Shamsie's telling, coupled with the appropriateness of the theme in an era when Muslim loyalties have come increasingly into question, adds relevance and dynamism. Moreover, the startling denouement takes what had until then been a solid, densely realised world, and transfigures it, in the most striking example yet of that mythic realism through which Shamsie's work grapples with the complex legacies of empire. Indeed, this novel itself has arguably been transformed too, becoming, thanks to contemporaneous political events in Britain, a kind of roman à clef: an instantaneous classic, encapsulating the outline of crucial debates about citizenship and rights. It might be useful briefly to contextualise *Home Fire* through one particularly salient controversy.

In April 2017, the then British prime minister, Theresa May, appointed Sajid Javid MP as home secretary. Javid was a former banker and the first Asian to hold one of the highest offices in the government. He was also the first Muslim to do so. During his fifteen months in the role, Javid caused controversy by a series of uncompromising statements on a range of issues concerning minority ethnic communities and asylum seekers. For example, when news broke of a child-grooming gang in Huddersfield, Javid spoke out against what he called 'Asian paedophiles', prompting *The Times* to note how Javid's 'heritage gives him a powerful voice against groomers' – rather compounding the idea that ethnicity was some kind of motive for such crimes.[3] Javid was perhaps as paradoxical a figure as Karamat Lone in the novel. When quizzed, he put some distance between himself and his Muslim roots, despite having been the victim of racism in the past. Interviewed on the subject of religion, Javid said, 'My own family's heritage is Muslim. Myself and my four brothers were brought up to believe in God, but I do not practise any religion. My wife is a practising Christian and the only religion practised in my house is Christianity'.[4] (In *Home Fire*, having been photographed entering a mosque for a relative's funeral prayers, the ever-astute Lone ensures that the next photo-op involves 'him and his wife walking hand in hand into a church' (*Home Fire*, 35), to assuage the fears of white, non-Muslim voters.)

One of the most high-profile cases Javid had to deal with as home secretary was that of Shamima Begum, a young British woman of Bangladeshi heritage who, as a teenager in 2015, had left her home in London with two friends to travel to Syria to join Islamic State fighters there. The girls were later married, becoming known in the press as 'Jihadi Brides'. In 2018, with her husband having been killed, a pregnant Begum expressed a wish to return to Britain. In response, Javid stated that British citizens who joined Islamic State would not be allowed to return to the United Kingdom and in February 2019 he revoked Shamima Begum's British citizenship. (The government claimed that she was a dual national, having citizenship of Bangladesh too, although this was disputed by the Bangladeshi authorities.) The decision to revoke Begum's citizenship was controversial, with opposition politicians, church leaders, and Amnesty International critical of the move, but it proved popular with the tabloid press and the public.[5]

The Begum case provided Javid, much like his fictional counterpart Lone, with the opportunity to look 'strong on security' (34). More than that, it raised important questions of citizenship. It is currently illegal under international law to make someone entirely stateless, but the decision to target those with dual nationality effectively creates a two-tier system: the citizenship rights of those with two British parents are guaranteed; dual nationals and the children of dual nationals are made more vulnerable.[6] This is a topic discussed in *Home Fire*, where Lone proposes a bill to 'make it possible to strip any British passport holder of their citizenship in cases where they have acted against the vital interests of the UK'. As he insists more than once, '"citizenship is a privilege not a birthright"' (198; see also 214).

Such moments make visible the perceived tension between Britishness and Muslimness in contemporary political discourse that lies at the heart of the novel. Lone comes to embody the strain, combining personal ambition and a desire to conciliate his party colleagues, voters, and the right-wing press. As a 'grandson of the colonised [who hopes one day to] take his place as Prime Minister' (214), Lone must forever be seen to be '[s]triding away from Muslimness' (52). He warns an audience of predominantly Muslim school children in Bradford: '"don't set yourselves apart in the way you dress, the way you think, the outdated codes of behaviour you cling to, the ideologies to which you attach your loyalties, because if you do, you will be treated differently – not because of racism ... but because you insist on your difference from everyone else in this multi-ethnic, multi-religious, multitudinous United Kingdom of ours'" (87–88). In the terms coined by Lisa Lau and Ana Cristina Mendes, Karamat 're-Orientalises' himself, cementing the perceived binary between good and bad Muslims by endorsing and inhabiting the existing loyal Muslim stereotype.[7] Yet, his divided nature is always bubbling to the surface; the tensions between Lone the father and Lone with his 'Great Office of State' (246) are never reconciled and he only learns the lesson about the value of family that Aneeka has sought to teach when it is too late to save his son.

Britishness-versus-Muslimness is seen always as a false dichotomy in *Home Fire*. In common with the earlier novels, it pits those who attempt to reach out across borders and boundaries against those who police them. In that sense, as its title might suggest, *Home Fire* continues Shamsie's exploration of home spaces from which people are forcibly wrenched, or which expel and reject them. Home is here exclusionary, complicated for second- and third-generation Muslim families by post-9/11 securitisation and the 'imperial melancholia' of contemporary Britain – that inability to come to terms with the historical consequences of owning an empire – identified by Paul Gilroy.[8] Shamsie is concerned to unpick facile ideological posturing, instead populating the novel with a wide variety of British Muslim principal characters whose backgrounds are painstakingly disclosed. Here, as in her earlier work, Shamsie is determined to show current events as the result of traceable historical factors, chief among which are the legacies of colonialism. In *Home Fire* this urge takes the form of a desire to fix events and characters in the 'real world' of the here and now which is, nonetheless, a product of history. It perhaps explains those extended accounts of some fairly minor characters' backgrounds in the first half of the book. Shamsie makes the point that almost everyone in the text, from Parvaiz and his sisters to Karamat Lone, and from the Pashas' Aunty Naseem to Eamonn's neighbours, the Rahimis, is – to borrow the old anti-racist slogan – *here* because Britain was *there*.⁹ As the plot unfolds, each of the protagonists have their personalities and life trajectories decisively shaped by a recalibration of Britishness that positions them precariously in relation to national identity. Ironically, this is clearest in the case of Karamat Lone who, despite doing everything he can to put distance between himself and his Muslim background, discovers that, for all his efforts to blend into the British establishment, he is only really tolerated until his mistakes can be turned against him by his political rivals.

Yet it is the Pasha family who experience most calamitously the clash between humanity and national citizenship rights. Presaging later events, the novel opens with a scene in which Isma is interrogated by airport security officers while trying to board a flight to begin postgraduate study in the United States. It is made clear that this is an eventuality for which she is well prepared. Isma has rehearsed with her sister answers to the kinds of questions she is likely to encounter, ensuring just the right level of compliance to satisfy her interrogator while suppressing the urge to use sarcasm or irony:

> The interrogation continued for nearly two hours. He wanted to know her thoughts on Shias, homosexuals, the Queen, democracy, the *Great British Bake Off*, the invasion of Iraq, Israel, suicide bombers, dating websites. ... [S]he settled into the manner she'd practised with Aneeka playing the role of interrogating officer, Isma responding to her sister as though she was a customer of dubious political opinions whose business she didn't want to lose by voicing strenuously opposing views but to whom she didn't see the need to lie either. (5)

In a further foreshadowing, as a student in the United States Isma produces a dissertation on the way the War on Terror is used to call into question Muslim citizenship in Britain. Debjani Banerjee describes how '[i]n her sociology class, Isma makes the point that depriving people of their rights had a long history in Britain: "the only difference is this time it's applied to British citizens ... who are rhetorically being made un-British"'.¹⁰ Yet despite her awareness, Isma is ultimately the more conventional of the two sisters, reporting Parvaiz's defection and counselling cooperation with the authorities. At the same time, her spirited response here and in a later face-to-face encounter with Karamat Lone where she pleads on her sister's behalf works against the stereotype of the passive Muslim woman.

Aneeka is an altogether more passionate, complex character. Isma's chance encounter with the son of the Home Secretary plants the seed of an idea by the nurturing of which Aneeka believes she may just be able to secure her brother's desired return from Syria. When they meet, she begins what is at first a simulated seduction, designed to win Eamonn's trust and thereafter his cooperation and influence. Aneeka is motivated at first less by romantic attraction than by the idea that proximity to the Home Secretary's son can help secure the safe return of her twin brother, Parvaiz, who has followed in his father's *jihadi* footsteps by ill-advisedly joining Islamic State forces in Syria, but who now wishes to return home. As the story progresses, Aneeka's and Eamonn's interests converge in a genuine love affair. The novel's preoccupation with secrets and simulation starts here as Aneeka stages a carefully choreographed courtship in which she is not above using her hijab – conventionally seen in the West as the symbol of Muslim women's submissiveness – as a tool of seduction. Shamsie here seems to say that stereotypes of 'the Muslim woman' are just that: reductive fixed traces that bear little relation to feeling, calculating, flesh-and-blood beings. Eamonn is baffled but fascinated by Aneeka's ability to switch in and out of 'the frequency of their relationship' (83). When he discovers her true motive for starting the affair, his anger is tempered by a continued inability to read this fascinating woman. Her professions of devotion prompt Eamonn to muse: 'It was what she'd say if she were still only trying to manipulate him. It was what she'd say if she'd really fallen in love with him' (100).

Along with secrets, the gap between appearance and reality and what characters can will themselves to believe is also explored. The description of the Islamic State confederacy with which the recruiter Farooq woos Parvaiz is part seduction, part sales patter. It consists of a precisely calibrated appeal to his target's social idealism. Parvaiz arrives for one rendezvous straight from fundraising for a volunteer-run library, set up after local council budget cuts have led to the closure of the local library service, allowing Farooq to sing the praises of the communal egalitarianism in Raqqa which stands in contrast to the slash-and-burn privatisation of modern Britain. Yet he is also able to pinpoint the personal bereavement behind Parvaiz's sense of aimlessness, promising that the Islamic State is a place where Parvaiz can 'speak openly about your father, with pride, not shame' (144). He passes Parvaiz a tablet and encourages him to scroll through pictures of male camaraderie interspersed with images of violent death and summary justice. Here Shamsie draws on one of *Home Fire*'s acknowledged source texts, Gillian Slovo's verbatim play *Another World: Losing Our Children to Islamic State* (2016), in which a radicalisation expert outlines the typical structure of Islamic State recruitment videos, beginning with visions of brotherhood and camaraderie but always including reminders of the violence necessary to maintain the utopia.[11]

When their brother Parvaiz first begins to spend time with Farooq, the tryst-like furtiveness of their meetings leads his sisters to believe he has found a girlfriend. Indeed, although Farooq can be understood as a father surrogate, there is still a decidedly homoerotic undercurrent to their relationship. He tenderly removes a splinter from the young man's palm; is encountered ironing in his underwear when Parvaiz pays a visit; and confesses, 'I've been thinking about you all day' (126). Yet sadomasochism is present too: Farooq makes as if to burn Parvaiz's hand with a hot iron and employs his henchman to restrain Parvaiz for hours in a stress position to simulate torture before dunking his head in water almost to the point of drowning. Parvaiz is complicit in this as he believes it allows him to share in that pain his father would have experienced when captured by coalition forces in Afghanistan. The violence grows exponentially when the scene shifts to Syria. Here Parvaiz, employed to make sound recordings for the militants, finds himself in a brutal hyper-masculine environment.[12] He is forced to record beheadings and is forbidden by a callous interpretation of Islamic modesty requirements from assisting an unveiled woman caught in the wreckage of a truck after it has been hit by a drone. The gap between Farooq's dreamland and the vicious, misogynistic reality of the Islamic State is one reason why Parvaiz is trying to escape and get back home when he is gunned down at the gates of the British Consulate.

States, whether Islamic or otherwise, are dangerous fictions. In the turning outwards to a transnational perspective one finds in her recent novels, Shamsie demonstrates that the backwash of history as it affects individuals is not contained by borders and boundaries. The transnational lens also gives us a way to understand Shamsie's decision to use *Antigone* as her template. The well-known story helps to establish an international, or world, rather than national lineage. Sophocles' play stages a human experience connected to a core set of dilemmas that repeat over time and in different contexts: loyalty to family versus loyalty to the state, the nature of justice and law, and so on.[13] This transnational artistic inheritance can be set against the fundamentalist nihilism of the Islamic State's caliphate and the exclusionary ethnic nationalism that Lone polices. In this way, we could say that Shamsie 'worlds' the novel – reinstates its connective power and the human (as opposed to economic) sense of globalised subjectivity – against those purist forces of nationalism and empire that are trying to narrow and capture (or eject) subjects who transgress established categories.[14]

Shamsie seems, in the later part of the novel at least, to conclude that straightforward realism is insufficient to this necessary task of worlding. This perhaps accounts for the striking formal rerouting of *Home Fire* in its later sections, taking us far from the grounded social detail of the early parts and into the realms of myth and the epic. *Home Fire* is divided into five sections each focalised by a different protagonist with help from an orchestrating omniscient narrator. Isma, Eamonn, Aneeka, Parvaiz, and Karamat Lone all get the chance to steer some part of the story, their perspectives providing a collage of attitude and experience. It is, however, noteworthy that while most of these voices relate events in a broadly linear way, the sections led by Parvaiz and Aneeka are significantly fragmented. Parvaiz's recruitment by Islamic State and subsequent longing to escape is a case in point; his desire to return home is narrated *before* we learn the cause of his disenchantment. The section thereafter moves backwards and forwards in time, filling in a sequence of actions and reactions, and trying to capture the more elusive strands of motivation that have led him to his fateful decision to join Islamic State. Aneeka's segment is even more radically disrupted, consisting of numbered parts made up of reportage, Tweets, tabloid smear stories, diary entries, and fragmentary meditations on loss, together simulating the cacophony surrounding the very public death of Parvaiz which compounds Aneeka's grief and sends her spinning towards a breakdown. An increasingly disjointed narrative, focalised by flawed but three-dimensional characters, has the further effect of steering us away from those stereotypes of Muslims that have proliferated since 9/11, calling our own reading practices and preconceptions into question. As Rehana Ahmed has noted, 'the novel distances its reader from its Muslim subjects and deflects an anthropological mode of reading which can limit western, non-Muslim responses to fictional representations of Muslims'.[15]

When Aneeka is prevented by Karamat Lone from bringing the body of her brother home to Britain, she travels to Pakistan to stage a vigil in a Karachi park in front of the assembled international media. It is significant that we see this climactic protest through the eyes of Karamat Lone – himself watching events unfold on a TV screen in his Westminster office. This enforced distance adds to the mystery of the tableau-like vigil, creating the conditions whereby Aneeka's actions as she receives the body and begins to grieve attain mystical power. Arrayed in the white of mourning she arranges what the novel, quoting Susan Sontag, describes as 'an iconography of suffering' (221), complete with a white sheet strewn with rose petals.[16] As Aneeka bends to see, once more, the face of her beloved Parvaiz, the distancing created by Lone's attempts to comprehend the spectacle – and the framing effect of the media images being beamed around the world – introduces an ambiguity about how to understand what happens next. Amidst the stifling heat of an impending dust storm, Aneeka breaks open the flimsy coffin and begins to explore her brother's remains in what almost seems a choreographed mime, but one where our interpretation remains provisional:

> The girl sat back on her heels, as if only now, at this moment, had she stopped to consider what she was asking her own eyes to look at. Or maybe she was waiting for what happened next: the yellow-brown wind picked up the plywood, and flung it into the air with a whipping sound.
> The girl lowered herself to her knees, placed her hands on the ground on either side of her and leant forward as a child might

examine some unknown animal found in the garden. Her brother, embalmed, looked *not right*. How else to say it? Dead.

She lifted a hand, looked at it as if she wasn't sure what it was about to do next, and watched as her palm came to rest on the forehead of what had once been her twin. The hand jerked away, settled back down. Slid along his skin towards his temple ... The hand lifted up again, moved down to the corpse's wrist, two fingers pressed against what would have been a pulse point. Her mouth opened and a small word or sound may have come out, nothing the mics could pick up. (223)

Immediately, the wind whips up, gathering into a howl that merges with the howl of grief escaping from Aneeka's mouth to create '[a] howl deeper than a girl, a howl that came out of the earth and through her and into the office of the Home Secretary, who took a step back' (224).

Media manipulation or some form of magic? The studied distance of perspective in the scene's focalisation leaves the reader to decide. We are left with the feeling that the inveterate politician Lone is most impressed with Aneeka's ability to stage a spectacle for the assembled press. Yet, with the elements too seemingly in rebellion, Aneeka's ritual calls back to earlier associations with uncanny powers. The infatuated Eamonn is perhaps an unreliable interpreter of Aneeka's unnerving ability to appear to him in times of need. Yet what are we to make of the title of the book he randomly plucks from the shelves of the café where he first encounters Isma at the start of the novel: '*The Holy Book of Women's Mysteries. Complete in One Volume. Feminist Witchcraft, Goddess Rituals, Spellcasting and Other Womanly Arts*' (17)? In the 'scene of martyrdom' (222) in the park we seem to be in the presence of something operatic, almost apocalyptic; the heightened registers of melodrama and the epic have seeped into what started out as a realist text. This apotheosis of Shamsie's mythic realism is of a piece with the obtrusive symbolism which increases towards the end, complete with a quasi-fairytale dead prince encased in ice – as efforts are made to prevent Parvaiz's corpse decaying – and incorporating sharpened auditory experiences, images of hot and cold, and the mixing of incongruous things: jam in the tea Lone makes himself; melting ice mixing with the dregs of wine in a glass – 'a foreign body in the ice', as the text says (237).

The novel reaches its climax with a tragic reunion of the lovers Eamonn and Aneeka. Eamonn has followed her to Pakistan only to find himself at the last minute approached by unknown assailants who strap a bomb belt to him. In front of the horrified gaze of his father (and a worldwide television audience) the lovers entwine in a final embrace with detonation seemingly imminent. This apocalyptic ending marks the culmination of the melodramatic turn: one final instance where Shamsie replaces the mundane registers of realism, the better to symbolise the suffering of those like Parvaiz and Aneeka deemed expendable by Western nations that are unwilling to be reminded of the extent to which they themselves may have set the conditions for radicalisation. Moreover, in calling back to classical forms such as the Greek tragedy, Shamsie seems to suggest that the restraint associated with the well-wrought novel is insufficient to encompass the rage and grief of the dislocated subject, cast into the wilderness by the operations of an impervious, unyielding power.

As Urszula Rutkowska has observed, 'Citizenship is a relationship between an individual and the state and not an individual and a government. Every Home Secretary is merely an impermanent guardian of that function of the state, and so the politicization of citizenship that has taken place in the "war on terror" will have long-term implications for how we understand rights'.[17] The political grandstanding and executive excess *Home Fire* illustrates, along with their implications for those non-white subjects who may fall foul of the authorities, are also on show in Shamsie's next novel, which begins long ago and far away from contemporary Britain.

*

Between the publication of *Home Fire* in 2017 and the appearance of Shamsie's next novel, *Best of Friends*, in 2022, Britain completed its withdrawal from the European Union. The exact terms of what became known as Brexit were a topic of huge contention, with legal and parliamentary disagreements clogging up the process of enacting the will of the slim majority who had supported withdrawal in the 2016 referendum. A constitutional struggle unfolded, with the Conservative-supporting *Daily Mail* denouncing as 'Enemies of the People' those High Court judges who ruled that the government required the consent of Parliament to give notice of Brexit.[18] The impasse led to the removal of one prime minister, Theresa May, and her replacement by another, the ebullient Boris Johnson, whose success in the 2019 election was accompanied by the rallying cry 'Get Brexit Done'. Faced with obstacles, Johnson's ruthless approach involved suspending recalcitrant members of his own party who questioned his tactics and proroguing parliament for the first time in over 350 years, a move declared unlawful by the Supreme Court.[19]

Brexit also took place at a time when increasingly tough measures were being advanced against migrants living and working in Britain. The so-called 'hostile environment', begun when May was home secretary, aimed to prevent undocumented migrants from accessing public services including housing and healthcare. Together with Brexit, the hostile environment marked a hardening of attitudes to outsiders, even those who had lived in the UK for many years and built a home and family life there. The turn from broadly welcoming migrants to open hostility is captured in an essay Shamsie wrote for the *Guardian* newspaper in 2020. Describing her involvement with the Refugee Tales collective of writers supporting those in indefinite detention, she noted how welcome centres for refugees had been turned into immigration removal centres with the aim of 'grinding people into submission' with a life so uncomfortable that leaving Britain would be a relief.[20]

Shamsie's unease with the political direction of travel in these years is shared by Zahra Ali, joint-protagonist of *Best of Friends*. Zahra is another of Shamsie's warrior women. In the second half of the novel, she has left behind a privileged upbringing in Karachi to become the campaigning director of the Centre for Civil Liberties (CCL) in Britain, a fictional version of the human rights organisation Liberty. In a profile interview, Zahra denounces the narrowing of rights which – along with the introduction of identity cards and the government's curtailment of the supposedly excessive powers of the courts – in her view poses a threat to democracy. Having grown up under the dictatorship of General Zia ul-Haq in 1980s Pakistan, Zahra has direct experience of authoritarian government. These two contexts, along with the novel's title, indicate how *Best of Friends* draws together some of the main preoccupations in Shamsie's writing to date: migration, citizenship, the tenuous nature of human rights, and the fragility of interpersonal intimacy. The main connecting threads here are the abuse of power by the powerful, the capacity of individuals for corruption, and the fraying of friendship under pressure from personal compromise and historical change.

Best of Friends has echoes of *Kartography* in the youthful closeness of its two central protagonists, Zahra and her fellow student at an elite co-educational school in 1980s Karachi, Maryam Khan. Maryam is the wealthy intended heiress of her family's luxury leather goods company. Her house in the well-to-do Old Clifton district is one step up from the comfortable but more modest Sea View apartment Zahra shares with her parents. Like Raheen and Karim in the earlier novel, Zahra and Maryam can initially find respite in their warming mutual confidence. They console themselves with the belief that 'whatever happened in the world you would always have this one person, this North Star, this rock, this alter ego who knew your every flaw down to your atoms' (*Best of Friends*, 28). Friendship appears more durable but also more reliable than the other kinds of relationship they see around them. Parents, although well-meaning, can be censorious, while boys are an unknown entity viewed with a combination of anticipation and trepidation.

Zahra harbours illicit sexual longing whereas the fourteen-year-old Maryam becomes the object of others' desires as her body develops. Bodily consciousness becomes acute for her, ending her participation in games of cricket with workers at the family firm. More socially diffident, Zahra nonetheless has the greater curiosity as the pair negotiate the challenges of teenage life under the watchful eyes of family and peers. In fiercely heteronormative Pakistan, the adolescent Maryam becomes a focus of prurient interest from males, while Zahra's more impulsive exploratory activities involve allowing passing drivers teasing glimpses of flesh. Both take turns to kiss a poster of George Michael on Maryam's bedroom wall, the singer's good looks attracting Zahra while his career trajectory – performing heterosexuality before later acknowledging his homosexuality

– provides a clue to Maryam's subsequent embrace of same-sex desire; as an adult she will establish a relationship with a female Nigerian sculptor and together they will bring up a daughter who is a result of sperm donation.

As girls in Karachi, the pair's awakening is accompanied by a voracious consumption of Western pop-culture items such as Jackie Collins novels, music by Madonna, Tracy Chapman, and Whitney Houston (arriving in Pakistan on mixtapes made by the students when holidaying abroad), and especially Hollywood teen romance movies. When the inevitable urges of youth clash with social repression, these films and their clichés become the primary means by which the students navigate their interpersonal and sexual development. Any eroticism is necessarily indirect in the heavily censored fayre they encounter on Pakistani television, so the looks and attitudes in US teen movies become a kind of code governing mating rituals that cannot be conducted openly. Shamsie has described how, like many teenagers in 1980s Pakistan, 'I watched Brat Pack/John Hughes films, repeatedly; I knew the Top 10 of the UK chart by heart; I cut out pictures of Rob Lowe, Madonna, a-ha from teen magazines and stuck them on my walls; I regarded the perfect "mixed tape" as a pinnacle of teenaged achievement ... I merely affirmed what every adolescent growing up, like me, in Karachi could tell you – youth culture was Foreign. The privileged among us could visit it, but none of us could live there'.[21] Such delights prove a welcome distraction from the violence of Karachi in the grip of the 'Kalashnikov culture' that was a result of the pilfering of weapons passing through Pakistan on their way to Afghani insurgents fighting against their Russian invaders. The students model their flirtations on those they view on the big screen to compensate for the inadequacy of Karachi school life. Zahra reflects: 'Without detention, how could there be *The Breakfast Club*? Without a school prom, how could there be *Pretty in Pink*?' (6). Nowhere is this debt more evident than at a sexually charged party Zahra and Maryam attend thrown by a friend's brother. Maryam stands 'one hand in a pocket, hip jutting out, as if posing for cameras', while '[b]eneath the frangipani tree a group of boys stood together, a flash of silver that was a hip flask adding something to their bottles of Coke. Everyone wanted something more than the school rules allowed' (92).

In its anatomy of female friendship, Shamsie's novel carries echoes of Elena Ferrante's celebrated Neapolitan Quartet (2012–15), in particular its first book, *My Brilliant Friend*. Both writers investigate the ways in which deep intimacy can coexist with intense but unspoken jealousy as two young women come of age. In *Best of Friends*, the boundaries between friendship and burgeoning erotic desire become cloudy when a love triangle develops between the two friends and Hammad, a vain but less well-connected classmate who initially sets his sights on Maryam but embodies sexual promise to the more receptive Zahra. Hammad plays the role of teen-movie bad boy, complete with gelled hair and leather jacket. Shamsie borrows and extends a brief scene in *My Brilliant Friend* where neighbourhood lotharios the Solara brothers try to persuade Ferrante's teenage protagonists to take a spin with them in their new car: a move fraught with dimly perceived danger and certain reputational disaster.[22] In *Best of Friends* things take an even darker turn when Hammad prevails on Zahra and Maryam to leave the party for a drive with him and his menacing older friend Jimmy in what becomes the decisive incident that resonates throughout the rest of the novel.

The girls are about to discover that the female body can be a target. Zahra's attraction to the frisson of sexual danger exuded by Hammad leads her to persuade Maryam to get into the car, but the exhilaration and freedom she feels as they hurtle onto the highway to a soundtrack of Michael Jackson songs is soon overtaken by fear. Jimmy speeds along with one hand on the steering wheel while the other begins to caress Zahra's cheek. Despite their protests, Jimmy drives the girls to the edge of the city, of safety, and of the known, stopping only to collect a consignment of contraband – perhaps guns, perhaps pornographic videos. When Maryam tries to intimidate him with her family's influential connections, Jimmy takes them to Napier Road, Karachi's red-light district. In this street of prostitutes, the reality of male power over women is laid bare: 'You could do anything to a girl here and no one would stop you if you had a car with tinted windows and a stereo system that drowned out all screams' (107). The girls are returned home physically unharmed, but the shameful connotations of their unchaperoned absconding leads to Maryam's disinheritance.

She will no longer take over the family firm as planned and is earmarked for a move abroad to a boarding school, thus interrupting her friendship with Zahra, who does not own up to being the initiator of their transgression.

The incident in the car is merely the most vivid example of the novel's preoccupation with the threat of arbitrary power and its violent use by the strong to cow the weak. General Zia's Pakistan is a country ruled by force and threats, in a model of national bullying that takes the place of functioning structures of justice and accountability. Zahra's father, a sports broadcaster, is visited by an army officer who strongly suggests he should use his television programme to praise the president. In an echo of Shamsie's early novels we learn that 'Zahra knew what it meant in Karachi when the powerful sent someone to "scare" their enemies. It was part of the character of the city, this other world of personal justice – messages delivered via fists and bullets and power drills' (131). Ironically, Maryam's own grandfather, known as 'the Patriarch', is not above paying gangsters to rough up those who cross him. He teaches Maryam the importance of power and is an admirer of the dictator Zia, as '[p]ower respects power, whether it comes from ballot boxes or bullets'. He advises his granddaughter: *'When you see the chance to increase your proximity to power, take it'* (62). In fact, in the family confrontation that follows the girls' safe return from their car escapade and concludes the Karachi section, there is a strong suggestion that Maryam's grandfather is disinheriting her less because her actions have brought shame on the family than because she has foolishly allowed herself to be made vulnerable to another's power. It is a lesson that Maryam will learn well.

Best of Friends explores what Zahra later calls 'the absolute terror of powerlessness' (303). Defencelessness is aligned with gender in Karachi but, as the text goes on to show, relative levels of power are a function of class and wealth too. After the car incident Hammad is expelled while the girls are free to continue their studies despite an act which could have brought their high-profile families and prestigious school into disrepute. Although the privilege of social status does not protect them from the menacing power of men, eliciting what they call the uniquely gendered torment of 'girlfear' (170), in later life Zahra and Maryam both enjoy the benefits associated with material wealth and connections. As the novel shifts to Britain in 2019 we find both women pursuing lucrative and high-profile careers with access to the perks that go with their class backgrounds, having seemingly put behind them the ordeal of their night-time drive with Hammad and Jimmy. Zahra is a leading civil rights activist with a rising profile and a circle of celebrity friends, while Maryam is a venture capitalist who has risen to be chair and major investor in a company that has developed a photo-and-video-sharing app called Imij, with added facial recognition technology.

Some early reviewers expressed reservations about the stark bipartite division of the novel into Karachi and London sections, with most preferring the experiential immediacy of the Pakistani elements. There were also concerns about the way the protagonists emerge as what Lorraine Berry calls 'two distinct archetypes of the "good immigrant": who are set on a crash course'.[23] Yet, one could argue that it is in the second half that the exploration of summary justice and the abuse of power, mapped onto class and ethnicity, achieves maximum impact. Thirty years have elapsed between events in lawless 1988 Karachi and the post-Brexit Britain of 2019, but democracy and justice are still subject to manipulation by those with contacts, wealth, and influence. While Zahra tries to stem the tide of anti-immigrant, anti-democratic legislation, Maryam is busy telling an interviewer that 'there is little to be gained by placing every kind of migrant in the same boat', and that she favours the admission to Britain of entrepreneurs who will make an economic contribution (147). As the British section develops, the complacent cruelty behind such discrimination will be made fully apparent.

Maryam fits well in a Britain where who you know is now more important than scruples or due process. Reflecting that '[e]veryone should be upfront about having exceptions to their principles if the price is right' (152), Maryam parks her socially liberal inclinations to cosy up to the right-wing government, ethnically diverse but keen to look tough on issues of law and order and immigration. Her awareness of class privilege is matched by an overwhelming desire to be accepted, or to buy her way into British elite circles. At a series of parties, she makes the acquaintance of the prime minister: a sharply satirical portrait by Shamsie of an individual not unlike the actual British prime minister at this time, Boris Johnson, with the same qualities of 'the jester, the charmer, ... [and] the lost boy', and guilty of the same loose Islamophobic language when talking about Muslims (222–223, 209).[24] With her instinctive knowledge of how the right connections can be exploited the world over, Maryam is able shamelessly to leverage her potential as a successful British-Asian entrepreneur whom the prime minister wants as the face of a post-Brexit publicity campaign extolling British business, in order to get him to call off an investigation into Imij's role in a bullying scandal that has hit the headlines. She giddily reflects on the ubiquity of elite corruption: 'How easy it all was once you were in this circle, how lightly everything could be done. Billion-dollar deals saved in a tone of banter. The classic elegance of a game unchanged across nations and centuries' (224). Maryam's access to such circles has been bought by her membership of the shadowy High Table group of elite donors who pay for access to the government. An internet search by Zahra when she discovers her friend is a member produces news stories about 'cash for access, cash for honours, arms dealers, the financial industry, Russian oligarchs, government contracts, tax breaks, secrecy, behind the scenes lobbying. "No links can be proved between the donations and any government policy" – naturally, that was the whole point' (255). Certainly, this list is cursory, and its implications not fully explored as extended attention is paid instead to the successful and well-remunerated professional lives and fluctuating adult friendship of Zahra and Maryam. Yet criticism claiming such detail is overdone[25] or that the novel is peddling a 'smooth globalism'[26] overlooks the darkening tone and increasing encroachment on this world of media appearances and glittering soirees by those marginalised in class and racial terms.

Cutting-edge technology, in the form of the Imij app, heralds a world where users can spare their blushes by quickly calling up the names of half-familiar acquaintances or keep their children safe on unescorted trips to the local park, but also where the potential for even greater and more constant surveillance poses a threat to the liberties of those already most at risk from unrelenting scrutiny by the eyes of power. As Michel Foucault, following Jeremy Bentham, reminded us long ago, the knowledge brought by surveillance *is* power.[27] Moreover, when combined with the ubiquity and reach of social media, Imij opens up the possibility for new forms of abuse. The scandal Maryam buries with the prime minister's help involves a thirteen-year-old Muslim girl driven to attempt suicide by bullies using the app. The campaign begun by the girl's father for sanctions against Imij is quashed by Maryam's use of a private investigation firm that uncovers evidence of his marital infidelity, while additional regulation that will detrimentally affect Imij's sale price is quietly ditched with prime ministerial assistance. In discrediting the girl's father, Maryam is merely acting out the lessons she has learned in youth: 'There'd never been any question of letting him win, but she hadn't wanted him destroyed, only defeated. Her grandfather would have been proud of her' (196).

Maryam displays the same ruthlessness, augmented by personal grievance and the desire for revenge, when Hammad and Jimmy reappear in London. Hammad picks up where he left off, initiating an ill-advised and unsatisfactory sexual liaison with the still-susceptible Zahra, while Jimmy is introduced to her civil liberties organisation as someone seeking indefinite leave to remain in Britain. Despite feeling the old revulsion, Zahra nonetheless agrees to help Jimmy by checking that his paperwork is in order. When Maryam hears of this, however, she decides the time is ripe for revenge. She uses the opportunity afforded by the Imij app to compile evidence of minor misdemeanours on Jimmy's part which are enough to sink his claim and lead to his detention and eventual deportation. In her shock at being the indirect cause of Jimmy's expulsion, Zahra resigns from her role with CCL. After a lifetime of shared secrets but even more keenly harboured resentments and minor betrayals, Jimmy's fate is sufficient to cause a seemingly final breach in Zahra and Maryam's friendship. A coda in the Spring of 2020 finds them still taking their regular walks through scenic spots in North London, but now in stony silence. Both have had a lesson in the fundamental unknowability of other people – even those to whom one has been closest. They are still linked by the shared experiences of their formative years but are now set firmly on divergent ethical and political paths.

Writing in the *New York Times*, Molly Young suggests that Zahra and Maryam are 'never convincingly tormented, only hassled' by the memory of the terrifying night-time trip with Hammad and Jimmy on which the novel hinges.[28] While this may be true, there is another character who pays the full price for being powerless in the wrong place at the wrong time. That figure is Azam, the Afghan baker's assistant who works across the road from CCL's office and whose application for indefinite leave to remain – 'the penultimate step on the road to English personhood', we are told (189) – is being personally overseen by Zahra. One of his visits to the office coincides with an attack by a racist, riled up by antagonistic right-wing coverage of CCL's activities, who hurls a carrier bag full of excrement into the office lobby. Azam punches the attacker in an impulsive act captured by CCTV in the street and quickly translated, via a social-media 'pile-on', into a story of a white man being attacked by a brown man. Azam's application is swiftly rejected and the last time Zahra sees him is when she visits the privately run detention centre where he is being held prior to deportation. Azam relates the primitive conditions in which detainees exist, six to a cell with a single toilet and no privacy: '"They want us to know we're animals to them, nothing better than animals"' (290). The interview room where they meet overlooks the yard where detainees are first brought in and Zahra notices that '[t]he door through which the detainees came and went ... had a sign over it saying, WE ARE ONE HAPPY FAMILY NO MATTER WHO WE ARE. What kind of mind', reflects Zahra, 'would think to put up a sign like that? The cruelty of this place made her set aside all the usual words – *immoral, unfeeling, playing politics with people's lives* – and land instead on *evil*' (288). Despite having made a life in Britain, Azam is to be separated from his family and sent back to Afghanistan. The last time Zahra sees him he is making plans to set up a bakery in Kabul using the skills he has learned in London. But, in a final crushing irony, the reader knows that the Afghanistan to which he is returning will soon be once more in the grip of Taliban repression, following the final withdrawal of American troops in 2021. For those like Azam, without wealth or connections, there is no 'way in' to Britishness, only exits from a country that no longer treats them as rights-bearing human beings.

At the heart of *Best of Friends* are what Chloe Ashby calls 'questions of responsibility, justice, power and ethics'.[29] Following on from *Home Fire*, the novel further underlines how the ability to set up, and move, home is determined by material affluence and connections. Zahra and Maryam have none of the social tenuousness that besets even a character such as Karamat Lone, but their meditations on the comparatively minor challenges of finding a sense of being-at-home in London are set in deliberate contrast to the Pashas and the Azams of the world who can inhabit a place and even believe it is theirs, but who are in the end much more easily cast out.

6.

Conclusion: Fiction, Form, and Freedom

Kamila Shamsie's novels have developed in ambition and sophistication and she is now one of the most perspicacious chroniclers of the modern world. Shamsie refuses to shy away from the long-term effects of history, eschewing those tempting byways where the novelist can focus on individual psychology or mere formalism to the exclusion of larger structures. Her work insistently calls upon us to connect past and present, just as it does the figures who populate its pages. Moreover, she is one of an increasing number of writers – among them Michael Ondaatje, Kazuo Ishiguro, Mohsin Hamid, Aminatta Forna, and others – whose work cannot be easily accommodated within the canonical boundaries of national literature.[1] Her novels derive much of their potency and appeal from this principled engagement with the world and the people in it, regardless of national origin, understanding them to be inextricably connected in the obstacles they face in achieving peace and justice.[2]

As Shamsie's reputation has grown, an increasing number of critics have begun to engage with her work.[3] Bruce King's 2011 essay 'Kamila Shamsie's novels of history, exile and desire' takes a synoptic view of the works produced up to that date.[4] King notes biographical influences on Shamsie's writing such as Agha Shahid Ali, her grandmother Jahanara Habibullah, and her aunt Attia Hosain. He credits Shamsie with putting Karachi on the literary map, but also remarks on her internationalism, identifying nods to Farsi, Persian, and Turkish literature. King locates the central theme of Shamsie's novels as 'the emotional discomfort that results from leaving the security of the past': a feeling encapsulated in her essay 'Mulberry Absences', where the reminder that since moving abroad she is never in Pakistan during the mulberry season induces a meditation on migration and loss.[5] The intertextual instinct that will later lead to what I have termed here mythic realism is also on display in these early novels in a self-consciousness which involves 'parodies of literary models, whether Shakespeare's plays, popular romance, or Sufi writings'.[6]

The early novels have drawn more critical interest in recent years. Writing of *In the City by the Sea*, David Waterman notes a concern with theories about the operation of time in a context where an authoritarian regime wields power over life and death.[7] He flags the text's central interest in what it calls 'pendular time' as a way of accounting for the relentless alternation of military and civilian governments in Pakistan. Waterman is right to note that the protagonist Hasan's family have a certain dilettante distaste for politics which makes them less than effective in combatting the cruelty of the president. It takes an outside force, the arrival of the Widow, to galvanise Hasan's imagination and also chart a broader, feminist resistance to the abuses of patriarchy. *In the City by the Sea* launches Shamsie's interest in boundaries and their transgression – here the boundaries between familial love and politics, and between fantasy and reality – barriers Shamsie's novels will test time and again.

Salt and Saffron has attracted a variety of critical approaches, being read through Marxist, feminist, and psychoanalytic lenses. Rehana Ahmed employs a materialist spatial analysis – also applicable to *Kartography* – in which the author's 'deterritorialized', cosmopolitan leanings are seen as obscuring the role of class in enabling or hindering the kind of transnational movement the protagonist Aliya enjoys.[8] (The perils of transnational movements by disempowered subjects are, of course, a central thread in Shamsie's later work.) For Munazza Yaqoob and Sofia Hussain, *Salt and Saffron* offers a realistic portrayal of the challenges faced by Pakistani women under a fiercely patriarchal social order. At the same time, though, Shamsie's work offers a way to break free from imposed ideals of women's roles and acceptable behaviour by projecting rebellious, strong-willed women who defy convention.[9] Khan Touseef Osman provides an interesting psychoanalytic reading of the novel through the idea of 'post-memory' and intergenerational trauma.

He suggests that the legacy of the rupture caused by Partition replays in subsequent generations, being connected, in *Salt and Saffron*, to class prejudice.[10]

The novels from the middle period of Shamsie's career to date are often read with one eye on the way they display a continuity of preoccupations with the early works, and another on how they anticipate later concerns. Ruvani Ranasinha teams *Broken Verses* and *Burnt Shadows* to explore resistance and religion. She sees the former's attempt to demonstrate the equal validity of religion and secularism being undercut by a tendency to privilege faith as inward rather than publicly performed; while the latter novel advances 'cultural Islam' and secular tolerance over religious belief, while nonetheless offering a 'means of articulating the tragic consequences and dangers of stereotyping'.[11] Cara N. Cilano has published two overlapping book-length studies of Pakistani writing in English. One looks at the 1971 war that led to the creation of Bangladesh, through the lens of fiction.[12] The other is a study of the idea of the nation state which argues that literature provides alternatives to officially sanctioned forms of identification.[13] Both demonstrate an excellent sense of historical background and they both also consider *Kartography*: the legacy of the 1971 war for characters in the contemporary 1990s timeline in one; and the alternative mapping of the city that pushes against conventional limits on identity in the other. (Caroline Herbert offers a similar reading of the novel's emphasis on heterogeneous identities, this time with an emphasis on the blending of mapping and Urdu lyric poetry.)[14] Cilano likewise sees *Broken Verses* as enacting the fragmentation of permitted identities both through the paranoia that overtakes Aasmaani when she receives the letters purportedly from the Poet, and through the queer forms of sociality embodied by Shehnaz Saeed's unrequited desire for Samina.

Burnt Shadows has proven increasingly attractive to critics, perhaps owing to its larger geographical and social canvas and post-9/11 frame-setting. Cilano suggests that *Burnt Shadows* makes an important distinction between 'privileged and unprivileged migrancies' as it distinguishes between chosen and enforced migration, suggesting the possibility of 'nationless belonging'.[15] The novel's attempt to establish a global, or 'world', aesthetic–political model – albeit in a context where writing about Muslims has become a sought-after commodity in the literary marketplace – is the subject of essays by Pascal Zinck and Ahmed Gamal, and book chapters by Daniel O'Gorman and Peter Morey.[16] A reading of *Burnt Shadows* is the centrepiece of Madeline Clements' chapter on Shamsie in her book, *Writing Islam from a South Asian Muslim Perspective*, which also engages with *Kartography* and *Broken Verses*. For Clements, Shamsie's 'decentred, Muslim female fiction of global unknowing' encourages the reader to suspend the rush to judgement, advocating instead intimacy with strangers and offering 'intense experiences of intra- and intercultural ... connection'.[17]

By contrast, comparatively little criticism has so far engaged with Shamsie's historical novel, *A God in Every Stone*. The standout interventions are by Maggie Ann Bowers and Tara Talwar Windsor. Bowers makes links between Shamsie's novel and Ondaatje's *The English Patient*, through the shared invocation of Herodotus and the emphasis on engaging with imperialism historically.[18] Talwar Windsor draws on Santanu Das's study of 'First World War culture' to claim that the novel allows for a form of commemoration inclusive of those marginalised histories that are usually ignored.[19]

Perhaps inevitably, *Home Fire* – with its striking take on topical questions of citizenship and belonging for Muslims in the nations of the West – has garnered most attention. New work is appearing all the time, so this short book can only point to indicative trends. Early on the scene was Claire Chambers, with a perceptive essay pointing to the role of sound and the auditory as central themes in the novel, taking forms including the soundscapes Parvaiz creates in London and the grim recordings of executions required of him in Syria. For Chambers, sound is linked to the political through the novel's demand that we listen to those minoritised subjects in contemporary Britain who rarely get a hearing.[20] Arin Keeble and James Annesley expand these enquiries to take in globalisation and multiculturalism. Offering a comparative reading of *Home Fire* and Zia Haider Rahman's *In the Light of What We Know*,[21] they see Shamsie's novel as tracing the core–periphery power dynamic that still governs globalisation and multiculturalism, noting in passing those metafictional elements that gesture towards the inevitable limitations of literary representation.[22] Four other essays directly explore the novel's political implications: Debjani Bannerjee shows how the text incorporates a narrowing state discourse about citizenship and cultural identity which reflects Western anxieties about 'radicalisation'; Urszula Rutkowska reads the novel against the backdrop of the Shamima Begum case, suggesting that Shamsie's narrative strategies make demands of the reader that run counter to the highly conditional hospitality offered by the modern nation; Lisa Lau and Ana Cristina Mendes apply their 're-Orientalism' theory, wherein Asians renegotiate their positions by inhabiting and thus reconfirming Orientalist conceptual frames and stereotypes (their main examples from *Home Fire* are Isma, Eamonn, and Karamat Lone); while Amina Yaqin, drawing on the theories of Achille Mbembe, notes the prevalence of necropolitical structures which render many of Shamsie's characters – including those in *Home Fire* – vulnerable to states of exception imposed by racist and patriarchal national forces, leading to exclusion or even death.[23] Perhaps the most astute essay of all – one that marries politics, form, and questions of readership most consistently – is Rehana Ahmed's 'Towards an ethics of reading Muslims: encountering difference in Kamila Shamsie's *Home Fire*'. Ahmed points to the emphasis on mediation and multiple viewpoints as an instance of the demand for an ethical, non-appropriative reading of the Muslim characters by a predominantly white, non-Muslim readership which often has an anthropological curiosity about cultural difference. The refusal to privilege any single perspective as somehow 'representative' of British Muslims 'disturbs "dichotomous divisions" between reader and subject, "saviour" and "victim", or "self" and "other"'.[24] *Home Fire* allows 'the reader access to a cast of British Muslims while at the same time denying the reader an appropriative consumption of their "Muslimness" through an increasingly exaggerated, melodramatic style which disturbs a reading of the characters as "authentic"'.[25] The melodramatic element is guaranteed through the use of Sophocles' *Antigone* as an organising framework. In outlining what she calls 'tragic form' in the novel, Naomi Weiss notes the theatrical traces in the text which rework classical features such as *agon* (a battle of speeches), *anagnorisis* (recognition), and the chorus. She also remarks on the presence of multimedia forms that produce a contestation of voices which the reader must negotiate and between which they must adjudicate. It is in the merging of form and politics that the power of *Home Fire* lies.²⁶

The intertextuality central to this merging has been present in Shamsie's work from the start but becomes more insistent and politically potent in the later work. In her turn towards what I have called mythic realism, Shamsie inscribes a recognition that realism can offer a backstory and surface details, but that something else is needed to convey the ongoing experience of expulsion from societies whose claimed liberal values are sometimes apotheosised in the realist novel form itself. She explores the implications of this insight through parodic reworkings, hyper-symbolism, and moments of surrealism and melodrama. Her novels are now 'global' in the sense that they are interested both in the effects of global history – in particular the aftermath of colonialism – and the flows of people that history has produced. In very different ways, her most recent works deal with the consequences of the global circulation of people and ideas, while nevertheless recognising that the realist novel emerged from within the same set of historical conditions which produced empire and globalisation. She is, likewise, a writer who is aware of the dangerous ubiquity of the stereotype. In a series of nuanced narratives, Shamsie acknowledges the temptation of reductive, shorthand ways of understanding people and crises, but remains alert to this danger and repeatedly foregrounds the inadequacy of the received account or the fixed, canonical version. In the same way, she eschews the burden of representation whereby she might be pigeonholed as a spokesperson for the Muslim peoples of Pakistan. Paul Veyret, quoting Amir Mufti, sees Shamsie's recent novels as engaging with the challenge 'of the "precarious balancing act between writing about the fundamental issues facing Pakistan [and, we might add, Britain] ... without playing to the metropolitan fascination with the spectre of Islam and stereotyped Muslim sensibilities"'.²⁷

Geography and history, time, space, and loss. These are the raw materials with which Shamsie crafts her fictions. She is a writer who understands that the challenge of doing justice to global experience is formal as well as thematic. Historical narratives and some novels, with their almost inevitable focus on the deeds of a few representative figures, frequently share a way of presenting the world which inadvertently takes a singular view for granted, paradoxically taming the polyphonic energies of the stories they tell through conventions such as omniscient narration and limited focalisation. By contrast, Shamsie often employs multiple perspectives and intertextuality in her fiction, providing alternative collage-like viewpoints on events and refusing the consolation of definitive answers. Her characters are always entangled, sometimes painfully, in the collective experiences of class, race, gender, and religion just as they are impacted on by past wrongs and present injustices. The variety of formal devices deployed in her novels reflects, and attempts to accommodate, this diversity.

Asked in an interview whether she was an optimist or a pessimist, Shamsie replied: 'I tend to be an optimist about human nature, but a political pessimist ... I think we're living in very, very scary times and we have to find ways of looking squarely at it and finding reasons for optimism'.[28] The sharing of stories and acts of narrative preservation that are the business of the novelist offer a way to meet the challenges of the present eye-to-eye and perhaps begin to find better, more humane solutions for the future. In doing so, they can extend the freedom of self-expression that some claim as a birthright but which is denied to those living precarious lives under authoritarianism or in fear of governments and majoritarianism. Fiction such as Shamsie's may offer a way to reimagine the connections that ideology tears asunder, thereby helping to construct a more inclusive, internationalist vision of the future. For Shamsie, the webs of history are still being spun.

Notes

1. INTRODUCTION: TRANSNATIONAL WRITER OF PAKISTAN

1 Kamila Shamsie, 'A long, loving literary line: Kamila Shamsie on three generations of women writers in her family', *Guardian*, 1 May 2009. https://www.theguardian.com/lifeandstyle/2009/may/01/kamila-shamsie-books-fiction-women
2 Muneeza Shamsie, 'Discovering the Matrix', *Critical Muslim 4: Pakistan* (October–December 2012), 165–176: 175.
3 Muneeza Shamsie, 'Sunlight and Salt: The Literary Landscapes of a Divided Family', *Journal of Commonwealth Literature*, 44:135 (2009), 135–153: 137.
4 Shamsie has testified to the profound influence of Agha Shahid Ali, both as a teacher and as a confidante who helped her to find her literary voice. See Kamila Shamsie, 'Agha Shahid Ali, Teacher', *Urdu Studies*, 17 (2002), 23–27.
5 'Young, gifted and multicultural: Granta's 20 authors under 40', *London Evening Standard*, 16 April 2013. https://www.standard.co.uk/lifestyle/london-life/young-gifted-and-multicultural-grantas-20-authors-under-40-8574848.html
6 Jochen Kürten, 'Writers protest the revoking of Nelly Sachs Prize from Kamila Shamsie', *DW*, 26 September 2019. https://www.dw.com/en/writers-protest-revoking-of-nelly-sachs-prize-from-kamila-shamsie/a-50590690
7 Bruce King, 'Kamila Shamsie's novels of history, exile and desire', *Journal of Postcolonial Writing*, 47:2 (2011), 147–158: 148.
8 In her book-length essay on the rise of a hardline Islam seemingly always at odds with the West, Shamsie describes how, far from being inherent in the Pakistani homeland for Muslims created in 1947, Islamic ideology soon became a politically expedient tool to cement together the disparate nation stretching from Balochistan to

East Bengal. See Kamila Shamsie, *Offence: The Muslim Case* (London, New York, Calcutta: Seagull Books, 2009), pp. 32–34.
9 For more on the history and cultural impact of the 1971 war, see Cara N. Cilano, *National Identities in Pakistan: The 1971 War in Contemporary Pakistani Fiction* (London: Routledge, 2011); and Ananya Jahanara Kabir, *Partition's Post-Amnesias: 1947, 1971 and Modern South Asia* (New Delhi: Women Unlimited, 2013). See also Daniela Vitolo, 'History, borders, and identity: dealing with silenced memories of 1971', in Aroosa Kanwal and Saiyma Aslam (eds), *Routledge Companion to Pakistani Anglophone Writing* (London and New York: Routledge, 2018), pp. 35–45.
10 See Farzana Shaikh, *Making Sense of Pakistan* (London: Hurst and Co., 2009), pp. 191–192.
11 Ayesha Siddiqa has famously dubbed this confluence of military and business interests 'Milbus'. See Ayesha Siddiqa, *Military Inc.: Inside Pakistan's Military Economy* (Karachi: Oxford University Press, 2007).
12 Saadia Toor, *The State of Islam: Culture and Cold War Politics in Pakistan* (London: Pluto Press, 2011), p. 85.
13 Ian Talbot, *Pakistan: A New History* (London: Hurst and Company, 2012), p. 137.
14 Munazza Yaqoob and Sofia Hussain, 'Changing Images of Pakistani Women in Kamila Shamsie's *Salt and Saffron* and *Broken Verses*', *Biannual Journal of Gender and Social Issues*, 11:2 (2012), 1–20: 1, 2.
15 Shamsie quoted in Mushtaq Bilal, *Writing Pakistan: Conversations in Identity, Nationhood and Fiction* (New Delhi: HarperCollins India, 2016), p. 148.
16 In addition to her novels, Shamsie has authored more than twenty short stories which have appeared in periodicals and charity publications. She has used these stories to expand her generic range, with many using magical or ghostly frames to explore themes such as migration, marginality, and the abuse of power. One of the most recent, 'Churail', was shortlisted for Britain's 2023 National Short Story Award. These stories also repay analysis but unfortunately lie beyond the scope of this short study.
17 Laurent Gayer, *Karachi: Ordered Disorder and the Struggle for the City* (Noida, Uttar Pradesh: HarperCollins, 2014), pp. 5, 23.
18 Cara N. Cilano, *Contemporary Pakistani Fiction in English: Idea, Nation, State* (London and New York: Routledge, 2013), p. 146.
19 Laurent Gayer cites a contemporary *Newsline* report suggesting that '"20–25% of the arms supplied are pilfered at different levels"'. Laurent Gayer, *Karachi*, p. 43.
20 See Samira Shackle, *Karachi Vice: Life and Death in a Contested City* (London: Granta, 2021), pp. xx–xxi.

NOTES

21 See Bina Shah, 'Paperback Writers', *Critical Muslim 4: Pakistan* (October–December 2012), 143–154: 148.
22 Yasmin Hameed, *Pakistani Urdu Poetry: An Anthology of the Post-Iqbal Urdu Nazm* (Lahore: ILQA Publications, 2022), pp. 16–17.
23 Amina Yaqin notes that '[y]ou will find examples of phrases and poems cited and quoted in a variety of places: television channels will devote hours of primetime viewing to cultural discussion programmes and performances of poetry and song; politicians will quote well-known poems in the certainty that their significance will be broadly understood; and even the drivers of trucks and rickshaws will have adapted poetic phrases painted on their vehicles'. Amina Yaqin, *Gender, Sexuality and Feminism in Pakistani Urdu Writing* (London: Anthem Press, 2022), p. 1.
24 Bina Shah, 'Paperback Writers', 148.
25 Sabyn Javeri (ed.), *Ways of Being: Creative Non-Fiction by Pakistani Women* (New Delhi: Women Unlimited, 2023), p. viii.
26 Gohar Karim Khan, 'Hideous Beauty of Bird-Shaped Burns: Transnational Allegory and Feminist Rhetoric in Kamila Shamsie's *Burnt Shadows*', *Pakistaniaat: A Journal of Pakistan Studies*, 3:2 (2011), 53–68: 56.
27 Muhammad B. Alam et al., 'In conversation with the renowned English fiction writers Kamila Shamsie, H.M. Naqvi, Omar Shahid Hamid and Osama Siddique', *The Wire: Exploring the World of Pakistani English Fiction*, 11 February 2018. https://thewire.in/books/four-pakistani-origin-writers-answers-questions-long-lost-on-the-minds-of-critics
28 Paul Jay, *Transnational Literature: The Basics* (Abingdon and New York: Routledge, 2021), p. 51.
29 Paul Jay, *Transnational Literature*, p. x.
30 Chimamanda Ngozi Adichie, 'The danger of a single story', TEDGlobal, July 2009. https://www.ted.com/talks/chimamanda_ngozi_adichie_the_danger_of_a_single_story?language=en
31 Rebecca L. Walkowitz, 'The Location of Literature: The Transnational Book and the Migrant Writer', *Contemporary Literature*, XLVII: 4 (2006), 527–544: 529. For more on how the material production and circulation of literature affect how it is valued, see Sarah Brouillette, *Postcolonial Writers in the Global Literary Marketplace* (Basingstoke: Palgrave Macmillan, 2011).
32 Walter Benjamin, 'Theses on the Philosophy of History, IX', *Illuminations* [trans. Harry Zohn] (London: Fontana Press, 1992), p. 249.

2. EARLY WORKS: *IN THE CITY BY THE SEA* AND *SALT AND SAFFRON*

1 Shamsie has described how Uncle Salman's fate was inspired by that of one of her relatives, a pro-democracy politician whom General Zia had placed under house arrest. Kamila Shamsie, 'Pop Idols', in John Freeman (ed.), *Granta 112: Pakistan* (London: Granta, 2010), 197–214: 202.
2 The Widow appears to be a composite of a number of women who rose to prominence contesting the worst excesses of General Zia's dictatorship in the 1980s, including the sister lawyers and civil society activists Asma Jahangir and Hina Jilani. For more examples, see Fouzia Saeed, *Tapestry: Strands of Women's Struggles Woven into the History of Pakistan* (Karachi: Lightstone Publishers, 2022).
3 David Waterman, 'Karachi's Fragmented Interdependence: Kamila Shamsie's *In the City by the Sea*', *Alizés: Revue Angliciste de La Réunion*, Faculté des Lettres at Sciences Humains (Université de la Réunion, 2013), 194–206: 194.
4 Attia Hosain, *Sunlight on a Broken Column* (New Delhi: Penguin Books India, 1992). See also Muneeza Shamsie, 'Sunlight and Salt: The Literary Landscapes of a Divided Family', *Journal of Commonwealth Literature*, 44:135 (2009), 135–153.
5 Rehana Ahmed, 'Unsettling Cosmopolitans: Representations of London in Kamila Shamsie's *Salt and Saffron*', *Journal of Postcolonial Writing*, 40:1 (2002), 12–28: 19.
6 For his celebrated, if controversial, assertion that all 'Third World Literature' tends towards national allegory, see Fredric Jameson, 'Third World Literature in the Era of Multinational Capitalism', *Social Text*, 15 (1986), 65–88.
7 The wit, elite focus, and romantic plot of *Salt and Saffron* infamously led Barbara Trapido to dub Shamsie 'our new multi-culti Nancy Mitford, a global girl who does love in both hot and cold climates', a quotation reproduced on the cover of the Bloomsbury edition of Shamsie's next novel, *Kartography*. It is a tag seemingly prompted by the upper-class social setting in these early novels, but which woefully misrepresents Shamsie's altogether more politically interrogative qualities and which, perhaps, took her a little time to shake off.
8 Munazza Yaqoob and Sofia Hussain have noted how Aliya and Mariam are quintessential early Shamsie heroines, 'revealing not only their anguish and anxiety about their own situation, but also their growing perception of themselves as individuals capable of self-willed action'. Munazza Yaqoob and Sofia Hussain, 'Changing

Images of Pakistani Women in Kamila Shamsie's *Salt and Saffron* and *Broken Verses*', *Biannual Journal of Gender and Social Issues*, 11:2 (2012), 1–20: 6.
9. Khan Touseef Osman, 'The Struggle of Memory against Forgetting in Kamila Shamsie's *Salt and Saffron*', *Crossings: A Journal of English Studies*, 11:2 (2020), 133–148: 136, 140.
10. Quratulain Shirazi, 'Tradition and Modernity in Kamila Shamsie's *Salt and Saffron*', *International Journal of Language, Literature and Culture*, 1:2 (2014), 23–27: 27.
11. Salman Rushdie, *Midnight's Children* (London: Jonathan Cape, 1981).

3. ECHOES OF THE PAST: *KARTOGRAPHY* AND *BROKEN VERSES*

1. Caroline Herbert, 'Lyric Maps and the Legacies of 1971 in Kamila Shamsie's *Kartography*', *Journal of Postcolonial Writing*, 47:2 (2011), 159–172: 168.
2. Kamila Shamsie, 'Bangladesh, Pakistan and India through a lens', *Guardian*, 6 January 2010. https://www.theguardian.com/artanddesign/2010/jan/06/bangladesh-pakistan-india-photography
3. Cara N. Cilano, *Contemporary Pakistani Fiction in English: Idea, Nation, State* (London and New York: Routledge, 2013), p. 144. See also Cara N. Cilano, *National Identities in Pakistan: The 1971 War in Contemporary Pakistani Fiction* (London: Routledge, 2011).
4. Stuart Hall, 'Constituting an Archive', *Third Text*, 15:54 (2001), 89–92: 92.
5. Claire Chambers, 'Kamila Shamsie', in Claire Chambers (ed.), *British Muslim Fictions: Interviews with Contemporary Writers* (London: Palgrave Macmillan, 2011), p. 221. In real-life Karachi, such open-ended remapping has been undertaken by the Orangi Pilot Project, established by the late activist Perween Rahman (1957–2013) to chart the sprawling city's unplanned (and poorest) districts and log their need for those basic amenities not yet provided by the civic authorities. See Samira Shackle, *Karachi Vice: Life and Death in a Contested City* (London: Granta, 2021), pp. 52–53.
6. Caroline Herbert, 'Lyric Maps', 161.
7. Farzana Shaikh describes how Zia's economic policies, including increasing privatisation, were coupled with a religious appeal aimed at creating a 'devout bourgeoisie' to shore up his position. Sonia's family seem to embody this newly religious middle class in *Kartography*. See Farzana Shaikh, *Making Sense of Pakistan* (London: Hurst and Co., 2009), pp. 108–109.

8 For more on how General Zia's Islamisation campaign shapes Shamsie's fiction, see Shireen Khan Burki, 'The Politics of Misogyny: General Zia ul-Haq's Islamization of Pakistan's Legal System', *Contemporary Justice Review*, 19:1 (2016), 103–119; and Amina Yaqin, 'Necropolitical Trauma in Kamila Shamsie's Fiction', *The Muslim World*, III:2 (2021), 234–249.
9 Kamila Shamsie, *Offence: The Muslim Case* (London, New York, Calcutta: Seagull Books, 2009), pp. 48, 49.
10 Saadia Toor, *The State of Islam: Culture and Cold War Politics in Pakistan* (London: Pluto Press, 2011), pp. 153–154.
11 Taha Kazi, *Religious Television and Pious Authority in Pakistan* (Bloomington: Indiana University Press, 2021), pp. 38–39.
12 Taha Kazi, *Religious Television*, p. 40.
13 Ali Madeeh Hashmi, *Love and Revolution: Faiz Ahmed Faiz, the Authorised Biography* (New Delhi: Rupa Publications, 2016), p. 8. Shamsie has acknowledged that, as a radical poet, Omi draws on characteristics of both Faiz and his contemporary Habib Jalib, commenting that the Urdu poetry they produced is 'an utterly populist and simultaneously politically crucial art'. See Claire Chambers, 'Kamila Shamsie', p. 225.
14 Between 1978 and 1983, Faiz lived outside Pakistan, travelling to cities across the world and settling for a time in Beirut in Lebanon, where he penned verses in support of the Palestinian cause at a time when Lebanon was facing an impending Israeli invasion to root out the Palestine Liberation Organization (PLO), which had based its operations in the country.
15 'Boond' is a word that carries the double meaning of 'drop' or 'abandon', but also 'drip', symbolically linking Aasmaani's own sense of abandonment to the novel's prevailing water imagery. Shehnaz Saeed's early career appears modelled on that of Shehnaz Sheikh, a popular television star in Pakistan in the 1980s who promptly retired from acting in the mid-1990s.
16 Ruvani Ranasinha, 'Religion and Resistance in the Work of Kamila Shamsie', in Rehana Ahmed, Peter Morey, and Amina Yaqin (eds.), *Culture, Diaspora and Modernity in Muslim Writing* (New York and London: Routledge, 2012), p. 205.
17 Cara N. Cilano, *Contemporary Pakistani Fiction*, p. 117.
18 Cilano notes how what she calls 'conspiratorial thinking' bleeds from the political realm, where many events in Pakistan are popularly read as a result of conspiracy, into the life-world of *Broken Verses* where the sudden appearance of the letters sends Aasmaani on a search for the truth so single-minded as to produce results bordering on paranoia. Cara N. Cilano, *Contemporary Pakistani Fiction*, p. 109.

19 See Kamila Shamsie, *Offence*, p. 51. In the light of this role for women poets it is interesting to consider why Shamsie has made one of her key protagonists a male poet. One reason might be because 'Riaz and (Kishwar) Naheed became prominent voices when they joined forces with the women's movement in Pakistan in the 1980s, but their poetry and politics remain lesser known than the voices of major Urdu poets such as Faiz Ahmed Faiz or Habib Jalib'. Amina Yaqin, *Gender, Sexuality and Feminism in Pakistani Urdu Writing* (London: Anthem Press, 2022), p. 15.
20 Farzana Shaikh notes that the Deobandi school, founded in Delhi in 1867, was concerned with 'the establishment of the political hegemony of Islam'. Farzana Shaikh, *Making Sense*, p. 109.
21 For the distinction between melancholia and mourning, see Sigmund Freud, 'Mourning and Melancholia', in *On Murder, Mourning and Melancholia* (London: Penguin, 2005), pp. 201–218.

4. THE WEBS OF HISTORY: *BURNT SHADOWS* AND *A GOD IN EVERY STONE*

1 Claire Chambers, 'Kamila Shamsie', in Claire Chambers (ed.), *British Muslim Fictions: Interviews with Contemporary Writers* (London: Palgrave Macmillan, 2011), pp. 209, 211.
2 Shamsie's father, Saleem, is the son of an Indian Muslim father and a German mother, which perhaps in part accounts for the focus on mixed-ethnic, cross-cultural unions in the novel.
3 Kamila Shamsie, *Offence: The Muslim Case* (London: Seagull Books, 2009), pp. 53–54.
4 For more on Bin Laden and Al Qaeda, see Fawad A. Gerges, *The Rise and Fall of Al-Qaeda* (New York and Oxford: Oxford University Press, 2011).
5 For more on the role of private security contractors in the War on Terror, see P. W. Singer, *Corporate Warriors: The Rise of the Privatized Military Industry* (Ithaca, New York: Cornell University Press, 2007); and Jeremy Scahill, *Blackwater: The Rise of the World's Most Powerful Mercenary Army* (London: Serpent's Tail, 2008).
6 Mohsin Hamid, *The Reluctant Fundamentalist* (London: Hamish Hamilton, 2007), p. 115.
7 Madeline Clements, *Writing Islam from a South Asian Muslim Perspective: Rushdie, Hamid, Aslam, Shamsie* (Basingstoke: Palgrave Macmillan, 2016), p. 144.
8 Cara N. Cilano, *Contemporary Pakistani Fiction in English: Idea, Nation, State* (London and New York: Routledge, 2013), p. 6.
9 Cara N. Cilano, *Contemporary Pakistani Fiction*, p. 224.

10 Ahmed Gamal, 'The Global and the Postcolonial in Post-migratory Literature', *Journal of Postcolonial Writing*, 49:5 (2012), 596–608: 598.
11 Peter Morey, *Islamophobia and the Novel* (New York: Columbia University Press, 2018), p. 209.
12 Michael Ondaatje, *The English Patient* (Toronto: McClelland and Stewart, 1992). Maya Jaggi notes the proximity of the two novels in Maya Jaggi, 'When Worlds Collide', *Guardian*, 7 March 2009. https://www.theguardian.com/books/2009/mar/07/burnt-shadows-kamila-shamsie-review
13 Maggie Ann Bowers suggests 'that *The English Patient* and *Burnt Shadows* can be read as companion novels in which the bombing of the cities of Hiroshima and Nagasaki at the end of World War II interpolates a deeper understanding of the problems of nationalism and colonialism at the hands of Europeans'. Maggie Ann Bowers, 'Asia's Europes: Anti-colonial attitudes in the novels of Ondaatje and Shamsie', *Journal of Postcolonial Writing*, 51:2 (2015), 184–195: 185.
14 E. M. Forster, *A Passage to India* (Harmondsworth: Penguin, 1985 [1924]).
15 For more on Ghaffar Khan, see Rajmohan Gandhi, *Ghaffar Khan: Nonviolent Badshah of the Pakhtuns* (New Delhi: Penguin Books India, 2017).
16 Salman Sayyid describes how the ancient empires of the Mediterranean, Arab, and Near Eastern worlds were mutually influential: 'The Persian imperial heritage has been plausibly traced from the imperial formations of the Assyrians of the sixth century BCE through the Babylonians, Achaemenids, Parthians, and Sassanids. In some case, the homage to previous empires was self-conscious … while in other cases it was implicit … The Roman Empire was philosophically grounded in the Roman republican tradition but also linked via *imitatio Alexandri* to Persian imperial tropologies'. See Salman Sayyid, 'Empire, Islam and the Postcolonial', in Graham Huggan (ed.), *The Oxford Handbook of Postcolonial Studies* (Oxford: Oxford University Press, 2013), p. 131. We can add to this list the subsequent Islamic imperial advances of the seventh and eighth centuries, themselves giving way in Western and Southern Asia to the European empires of the eighteenth, nineteenth, and twentieth centuries.
17 Claire Chambers, 'Kamila Shamsie', p. 216.
18 *A God in Every Stone* shares a sense of the symbolic significance of such diverse traces with Nadeem Aslam's 2009 novel *The Wasted Vigil* (London: Faber and Faber, 2009).
19 For more on the traveller, writer, administrator, and archaeologist Gertrude Bell, see Janet Wallach, *Desert Queen: The Extraordinary Life of Gertrude Bell* (New York: Anchor Books, 2005).

NOTES

20 Madeline Clements has noted how one effect of Shamsie's treatment of those Muslim women traditionally seen by the West as oppressed – including those who wear the veil or burqa – is to contest the exoticism surrounding what Gayatri Spivak has famously termed the silent subaltern, by allowing religious and culturally inflected choices to exist on their own terms without the need to explain them away or make them somehow more palatable: 'In Shamsie's countering fiction, the potentially repressive causes of South Asian "Muslim" female behaviours which trouble a "liberal" West are enquired into but left hanging'. Madeline Clements, *Writing Islam*, p. 130.
21 Vladimir Propp, *Morphology of the Folktale* (Second Edition) [trans. Laurence Scott] (Austin: University of Texas, 1968), pp. 36–37.
22 See Tara Talwar Windsor, 'Marginalized Memories and Multi-Layered Narratives of the Great War in Kamila Shamsie's *A God in Every Stone*', *Forum for Modern Language Studies*, 56:2 (2020), 229–246: 232.
23 Tara Talwar Windsor, 'Marginalized Memories', 230, 234.

5. AT HOME IN THE WORLD: *HOME FIRE* AND *BEST OF FRIENDS*

1 Kamila Shamsie, 'Everest is Climbed', in Sabyn Javeri (ed.), *Ways of Being: Creative Non-Fiction by Pakistani Women* (New Delhi: Women Unlimited, 2023), pp. 84–85. See also Vanessa Thorpe, 'Kamila Shamsie: "Being a UK citizen makes me feel more able to take part in the conversation"', *Observer*, 27 August 2017. https://www.theguardian.com/books/2017/aug/27/kamila-shamsie-home-fire-man-booker-longlisted-author-interview
2 For a consideration of the way in which *Home Fire* incorporates some of the formal as well as thematic elements of Sophocles' *Antigone*, see Naomi Weiss, 'Tragic Form in Kamila Shamsie's *Home Fire*', *Classical Reception Journal*, 14:2 (2022), 240–263.
3 In fact, Shamsie interviewed Sajid Javid on BBC Radio 4's *Today* programme and quizzed him about some of his statements on 26 December 2018. For the genesis of the character of Karamat Lone and his relationship to existing British-Muslim politicians, see Kamila Shamsie, 'True story: Kamila Shamsie on predicting the rise of Sajid Javid', *Guardian*, 3 May 2018. https://www.theguardian.com/books/booksblog/2018/may/03/true-story-kamila-shamsie-on-predicting-the-rise-of-sajid-javid
4 Alice Fuller, 'A Little Faith: What Religion is Sajid Javid', *Sun*, 28 June 2021. https://www.thesun.co.uk/news/15415540/what-religion-is-sajid-javid/

5 Urszula Rutkowska considers the principles involved in stripping people of their citizenship in the light of the Shamima Begum case and notes how *Home Fire*, through its polyphonic, interrogative form, asks questions of the reader which may draw attention to their own ideological interpretative biases where characters are concerned. See Urszula Rutkowska, 'The Political Novel in our still-evolving reality: Kamila Shamsie's *Home Fire* and the Shamima Begum case', *Textual Practice*, 36:6 (2022), 871–888.

6 The history of such measures, including the recent erosion of citizenship rights for those born outside the United Kingdom, is the subject of a 2018 *Guardian* newspaper article by Shamsie. See Kamila Shamsie, 'Exiled: The Disturbing Story of a Citizen Made unBritish', *Guardian*, 17 November 2018.

7 Lisa Lau and Ana Cristina Mendes, 'Twenty-First Century Antigones: The Postcolonial Woman Shaped by 9/11 in Kamila Shamsie's *Home Fire*', *Studies in the Novel*, 53:1 (2021), 54–68: 62–63.

8 See Paul Gilroy, *After Empire: Melancholia or Convivial Culture?* (Abingdon: Routledge, 2004).

9 See Ian Sanjay Patel, *We're Here Because You Were There: Immigration and the End of Empire* (London: Verso Books, 2022).

10 Debjani Banerjee, 'From Cheap Labour to Overlooked Citizens: Looking for British Muslim Identities in Kamila Shamsie's *Home Fire*', *South Asian Review*, 41:3–4 (2020), 288–302: 294.

11 See Gillian Slovo, *Another World: Losing Our Children to Islamic State* (London: Oberon Books, 2016), p. 31. The expert appears to be modelled on Charlie Winter, a Senior Research Fellow working on radicalisation at King's College London. Shamsie acknowledges the debt in an interview: Vanessa Thorpe, 'Kamila Shamsie'.

12 For more on what she calls 'the susurrus of homoeroticism' and the edge of sadomasochism between Parvaiz and Farooq in the context of an exploration of the novel's soundscapes, see Claire Chambers, 'Sound and Fury: Kamila Shamsie's *Home Fire*', *The Massachusetts Review*, 59:2 (2018), 202–219: 207, 209.

13 Naomi Weiss notes how *Antigone* has proved a popular target for rewritings over the years, '[f]rom Jean Anouilh's *Antigone* (1944) to Athol Fugard's *The Island* with John Kani and Winston Ntshona (1976) to Theater of War's *Antigone in Ferguson* (2016). Such plays and productions have often used Sophocles' tragedy to explore ways for the oppressed and powerless to publicly counter their powerful oppressors'. Naomi Weiss, 'Tragic Form', 243.

14 For more on the idea of 'worlding' the novel, see Djelal Kadir, 'To World, to Globalize – Comparative Literature's Crossroads', *Comparative Literary Studies*, 41:1 (2004), 1–9. Kadir advocates treating the term 'world' – as in World Literature – as a verb in order to

attend to the forces which are constructing the category. I have suggested elsewhere that this insight opens up the possibility for alternative 'worldings' of the kind one finds in the transnational post-9/11 fictions of Shamsie and Nadeem Aslam. See Peter Morey, *Islamophobia and the Novel* (New York: Columbia University Press, 2018), pp. 191–192.
15 Rehana Ahmed, 'Towards an ethics of reading Muslims: encountering difference in Kamila Shamsie's *Home Fire*', *Textual Practice*, 35:7 (2021), 1145–1161: 1148.
16 Susan Sontag, *Regarding the Pain of Others* (London: Penguin, 2003), p. 34.
17 Urszula Rutkowska, 'The Political Novel', p. 886.
18 'Enemies of the People: Fury over "out of touch" judges who have "declared war on democracy" by defying 17.4m Brexit voters and who could trigger constitutional crisis', *Daily Mail*, 3 November 2016. https://www.dailymail.co.uk/news/article-3903436/Enemies-people-Fury-touch-judges-defied-17-4m-Brexit-voters-trigger-constitutional-crisis.html
19 House of Commons Library, 'The Prorogation Dispute of 2019: one year on'. https://commonslibrary.parliament.uk/research-briefings/cbp-9006/
20 Kamila Shamsie, 'The UK once welcomed refugees – now we detain them indefinitely. It must end', *Guardian*, 4 July 2020. https://www.theguardian.com/books/2020/jul/04/the-uk-once-welcomed-refugees-now-we-detain-them-indefinitely-it-must-end
21 Kamila Shamsie, 'Pop Idols', in John Freeman (ed.), *Granta 112: Pakistan* (London: Granta, 2010), 197–214: 199. In the same essay, Shamsie writes of the attraction of cruising along in a car with a group of friends, singing along to 'mixed tapes' of Western music, anticipating the scene in *Best of Friends* in which Zahra and Maryam find themselves on a joyride that quickly turns menacing.
22 Elena Ferrante, *My Brilliant Friend* [trans. Ann Goldstein] (London: Europa Editions, 2012), pp. 134–135.
23 Lorraine Berry, 'Review: Kamila Shamsie's new novel asks: Should friendship transcend politics?' *Los Angeles Times*, 27 September 2022. https://www.latimes.com/entertainment-arts/books/story/2022-09-27/review-kamila-shamsie-new-novel-asks-should-friendship-always-transcend-politics
24 Shortly before he became prime minister, Boris Johnson notoriously claimed that burqa-wearing women looked like letterboxes, provoking an immediate condemnatory backlash. Johnson's comments were reportedly followed by a rise in Islamophobic incidents targeting women. Boris Johnson, 'Denmark has got it wrong. Yes, the burka [sic] is oppressive and ridiculous – but that's

no reason to ban it', *Daily Telegraph*, 5 August 2018. https://www.telegraph.co.uk/news/2018/08/05/denmark-has-got-wrong-yes-burka-oppressive-ridiculous-still/; see also PA Mediapoint and *Press Gazette*, 'Boris Johnson's Telegraph column comparing Muslim women with "letterboxes" led to Islamophobic "spike"', *Press Gazette*, 2 September 2019. https://pressgazette.co.uk/news/boris-johnson-telegraph-column-muslim-women-letterboxes-bank-robbers-spike-islamophobic-incidents/#:~:text=In%20the%20Telegraph%20article%2C%20published,appointed%20Prime%20Minister%20last%20month

25 Kelsey S. Mann, '"Best of Friends" Review: An Underwhelming Tale of Childhood Friendship', *Harvard Crimson*, 15 November 2022. https://www.thecrimson.com/article/2022/11/15/best-of-friends-review-kamila-shamsie-2022/

26 Tanjil Rashid, 'Best of Friends by Kamila Shamsie review – Karachi to London', *Guardian*, 23 September 2022. https://www.theguardian.com/books/2022/sep/23/best-of-friends-by-kamila-shamsie-review-karachi-to-london

27 Michel Foucault, *Discipline and Punish: The Birth of the Prison* (London: Penguin, 1991 [1979]).

28 Molly Young, 'A Study of Friendship Where the Past Really Is Another Country', *New York Times*, 27 September 2022. https://www.nytimes.com/2022/09/27/books/review/best-of-friends-kamila-shamsie.html

29 Chloe Ashby, 'A complicated bond: The Best of Friends, by Kamila Shamsie. Reviewed', *Spectator*, 24 September 2022. https://www.spectator.co.uk/article/a-complicated-bond-the-best-of-friends-by-kamila-shamsie-reviewed/

6. CONCLUSION: FICTION, FORM, AND FREEDOM

1 Selma Dabbagh, 'Selma Dabbagh on *A God in Every Stone*', *Wasafiri*, 17 January 2015. https://www.wasafiri.org/article/selma-dabbagh-on-a-god-in-every-stone/

2 As Amina Yaqin puts it: 'Her writing underlines the growing void regarding citizenship rights within existing democracies and the need for a more ethical democratic future informed by planetary justice'. Amina Yaqin, 'Necropolitical Trauma in Kamila Shamsie's Fiction', *The Muslim World*, III:2 (2021), 234–249: 236.

3 At the time of writing, no scholarly criticism on *Best of Friends* (2022) has yet appeared. We can be sure this state of affairs will change very soon.

4   Bruce King, 'Kamila Shamsie's novels of history, exile and desire', *Journal of Postcolonial Writing*, 47:2 (2011), 147–158.
5   Bruce King, 'Kamila Shamsie's novels', 147.
6   Bruce King, 'Kamila Shamsie's novels', 149.
7   David Waterman, 'Karachi's Fragmented Interdependence: Kamila Shamsie's *In the City by the Sea*', *Alizés: Revue Angliciste de La Réunion*, Faculté des Lettres at Sciences Humains (Université de la Réunion, 2013), 194–206.
8   Rehana Ahmed, 'Unsettling Cosmopolitans: Representations of London in Kamila Shamsie's *Salt and Saffron*', *Journal of Postcolonial Writing*, 40:1 (2002), 12–28.
9   Munazza Yaqoob and Sofia Hussain, 'Changing Images of Pakistani Women in Kamila Shamsie's *Salt and Saffron* and *Broken Verses*', *Biannual Journal of Gender and Social Issues*, 11:2 (2012).
10 Khan Touseef Osman, 'The Struggle of Memory against Forgetting in Kamila Shamsie's *Salt and Saffron*', *Crossings: A Journal of English Studies*, 11:2 (2020), 133–148.
11 Ruvani Ranasinha, 'Religion and Resistance in the Work of Kamila Shamsie', in Rehana Ahmed, Peter Morey, and Amina Yaqin (eds.), *Culture, Diaspora and Modernity in Muslim Writing* (New York and London: Routledge, 2012), pp. 200–214: 212.
12 Cara N. Cilano, *National Identities in Pakistan: The 1971 War in Contemporary Pakistani Fiction* (London: Routledge, 2011).
13 Cara N. Cilano, *Contemporary Pakistani Fiction in English: Idea, Nation, State* (London and New York: Routledge, 2013).
14 Caroline Herbert, 'Lyric maps and the legacies of 1971 in Kamila Shamsie's *Kartography*', *Journal of Postcolonial Writing*, 47:2 (2011), 159–172.
15 Cara N. Cilano, *Contemporary Pakistani Fiction*, p. 222.
16 Pascal Zinck, 'Eyeless in Guantanamo: Vanishing Horizons in Kamila Shamsie's *Burnt Shadows*', *Commonwealth*, 33:1 (2010), 45–54; Ahmed Gamal, 'The Global and the Postcolonial in Post-Migratory Literature', *Journal of Postcolonial Writing*, 49:5 (2012), 596–608; Daniel O'Gorman, *Fictions of the War on Terror: Difference and the Transnational 9/11 Novel* (London: Palgrave Macmillan, 2015), pp. 112–141; Peter Morey, *Islamophobia and the Novel* (New York: Columbia University Press, 2018), pp. 183–210.
17 Madeline Clements, *Writing Islam from a South Asian Muslim Perspective: Rushdie, Hamid, Aslam, Shamsie* (London: Palgrave Macmillan, 2016), pp. 123–124.
18 Maggie Ann Bowers, 'Asia's Europes: Anti-colonial attitudes in the novels of Ondaatje and Shamsie', *Journal of Postcolonial Writing*, 51:2 (2015), 184–195.

19 Tara Talwar Windsor, 'Marginalized Memories and Multi-Layered Narratives of the Great War in Kamila Shamsie's *A God in Every Stone*', *Forum for Modern Language Studies*, 56:2 (2020), 229–246. See also Santanu Das, *India, Empire, and First World War Culture: Writings, Images, and Songs* (Cambridge: Cambridge University Press, 2018).
20 Claire Chambers, 'Sound and Fury: Kamila Shamsie's *Home Fire*', *The Massachusetts Review*, 59:2 (2018), 202–219. See also Claire Chambers, *Making Sense of Contemporary British Novels* (London: Palgrave Macmillan, 2019), pp. 169–211.
21 Zia Haider Rahman, *In the Light of What We Know* (New York: Farrar, Strauss and Giroux, 2014).
22 Arin Keeble and James Annesley, 'Globalism, Multiculturalism and Violence in Zia Haider Rahman's *In the Light of What We Know* (2014) and Kamila Shamsie's *Home Fire* (2017)', *Parallax*, 27:1 (2021), 79–97.
23 Debjani Bannerjee, 'From Cheap Labour to Overlooked Citizens: Looking for British Muslim Identities in Kamila Shamsie's *Home Fire*', *South Asian Review*, 41:3–4 (2020), 288–302; Urszula Rutkowska, 'The Political Novel in our still-evolving reality: Kamila Shamsie's *Home Fire* and the Shamima Begum case', *Textual Practice*, 36:6 (2022), 871–888; Lisa Lau and Ana Cristina Mendes, 'Twenty-First-Century Antigones: The Postcolonial Woman Shaped by 9/11 in Kamila Shamsie's *Home Fire*', *Studies in the Novel*, 53:1 (2021), 54–68; Amina Yaqin, 'Necropolitical Trauma', 234–249.
24 Rehana Ahmed, 'Towards an ethics of reading Muslims: encountering difference in Kamila Shamsie's *Home Fire*', *Textual Practice*, 35:7 (2021), 1145–1161: 1147.
25 Rehana Ahmed, 'Towards an ethics', 1159.
26 Naomi Weiss, 'Tragic Form in Kamila Shamsie's *Home Fire*', *Classical Reception Journal*, 14:2 (2022), 240–263. The lineaments of *Antigone* also shape Abbie Jukes's recent primer on *Home Fire*, a publication which testifies to the novel's presence on school as well as university syllabi. Abbie Jukes, *An Introduction to Kamila Shamsie's* Home Fire (London: Greenwich Exchange, 2023).
27 Paul Veyret, 'Fractured territories: Deterritorializing the contemporary Pakistani novel in English', *Journal of Commonwealth Literature*, 56:2 (2018), 307–321: 311.
28 Claire Armitstead, 'Kamila Shamsie: "We have to find reasons for optimism"', *Guardian*, 8 June 2018. https://www.theguardian.com/books/2018/jun/08/kamila-shamsie-we-have-to-find-reasons-for-optimism-home-fire

Select Bibliography

Published Novels by Kamila Shamsie (with first editions by date of publication)

In the City by the Sea (London: Granta, 1998).
Salt and Saffron (London: Bloomsbury, 2000).
Kartography (London: Bloomsbury, 2002).
Broken Verses (London: Bloomsbury, 2005).
Burnt Shadows (London: Bloomsbury, 2009).
A God in Every Stone (London: Bloomsbury, 2014).
Home Fire (London: Bloomsbury, 2017).
Best of Friends (London: Bloomsbury, 2022).

Short Stories (in chronological order)

'Horatio's story', in Kate Pullinger (ed.), *Shoe Fly Baby: The Asham Award Short Story Collection* (London: Bloomsbury, 2004).
'Hieroglyphics of the Dead', in Rajeev Balasubramaniyan and Courttia Newland (eds.), *Tell Tales: The Anthology of Short Stories, Volume 2* (London: Flipped Eye Publishing, 2005).
'Miscarriage', in Anna Wilson (ed.), *Lebanon, Lebanon* (London: Saqi Books, 2006).
'Surface of Glass', in Muneeza Shamsie (ed.), *And the World Changed: Contemporary Stories by Pakistani Women* (New York: The Feminist Press, 2008).
'The Desert Torso', in Mark Ellingham and Peter Florence (eds.), *Ox-Tales: Air* (London: Profile Books, 2009).
'9/11 Stories: Our Dead, Your Dead', *Guardian*, 2 September 2011.
'Gold Medal Day', in Mary Morris (ed.), *Road Stories: New Stories Inspired by Exhibition Road* (Royal Borough of Kensington and Chelsea/Dream, 2012).
'War Letters' – multimedia short story and film with Grid Iron Theatre Company and the Edinburgh International Book Festival (2014).

Untitled in the 'Six Shorts' section of John Freeman (ed.), *Freeman's: The Best New Writing on Arrival* (2015).

'Mir Aslam of Kolachi', in Daniel Hahn and Margarita Valencia (eds.), *Lunatics, Lovers and Poets: Twelve Stories after Cervantes and Shakespeare* (Sheffield: And Other Stories, 2016).

'The Girl Next Door', in Sabrina Mahfouz (ed.), *Things I Would Tell You: British Muslim Women Write* (London: Saqi Books, 2017).

'Foreboding', in *Eight Ghosts: The English Heritage Book of New Ghost Stories* (London: September Publishing, 2017).

'The Lover's Tale', in David Herd and Anna Pincus (eds.), *Refugee Tales II* (Manchester: Comma Press, 2017).

'The Congregation', in Mahvesh Murad and Jared Shurin (eds.), *The Djinn Falls in Love and Other Stories* (London: REBCA, 2017).

'A Game of Chess', in Magda Raczynska and Becky Harrison (eds.), *Conradology: A Celebration of the Work of Joseph Conrad* (Manchester: Comma Press, 2017).

'Savage', in Ra Page (ed.), *Resist: Stories of Uprising* (Manchester: Comma Press, 2019).

'The Walk', *New York Times Magazine*, 7 July 2020.

Duckling: A Fairytale Revolution [illustrator Laura Barrett] (London: Penguin, 2020).

'Churail', in *Furies: The Virago Book of Wild Writing* (London: Virago, 2023).

Selected Journalism, Essays, and Non-Fiction (chronological)

'Mulberry Absences', in Muneeza Shamsie (ed.), *Leaving Home: Towards a New Millennium* (Karachi: Oxford University Press, 2001), pp. 394–397.

'Agha Shahid Ali, Teacher', *Urdu Studies*, 17 (2002), 23–27.

'More Honest than the Facts', *Guardian*, 3 July 2007.

'A long, loving literary line: Kamila Shamsie on three generations of women writers in her family', *Guardian*, 1 May 2009.

Offence: The Muslim Case (London, New York, Calcutta: Seagull Books, 2009).

'Pop Idols', in John Freeman (ed.), *Granta 112: Pakistan* (London: Granta, 2010), 197–214.

'Bangladesh, Pakistan and India through a lens', *Guardian*, 6 January 2010.

'Kamila Shamsie on leaving and returning to Karachi', *Guardian*, 13 March 2010.

'True story: Kamila Shamsie on predicting the rise of Sajid Javid', *Guardian*, 3 May 2018.

'Exiled: The Disturbing Story of a Citizen Made unBritish', *Guardian*, 17 November 2018.

'The UK once welcomed refugees – now we detain them indefinitely. It must end', *Guardian*, 4 July 2020.

'Everest is Climbed', in Sabyn Javeri (ed.), *Ways of Being: Creative Non-Fiction by Pakistani Women* (New Delhi: Women Unlimited, 2023), pp. 84–85.

Selected Interviews (alphabetical)

Alam, Muhammad B., et al., 'In conversation with the renowned English fiction writers Kamila Shamsie, H.M. Naqvi, Omar Shahid Hamid and Osama Siddique', *The Wire: Exploring the World of Pakistani English Fiction*, 11 February 2018.

Allfree, Claire, 'Kamila Shamsie: "The government's anti-migrant position is outflanking that of the public"', *Independent*, 27 September 2022. https://www.independent.co.uk/arts-entertainment/books/features/kamila-shamsie-interview-book-best-of-friends-b2175291.html

Chambers, Claire, 'Kamila Shamsie', in Claire Chambers (ed.), *British Muslim Fictions: Interviews with Contemporary Writers* (London: Palgrave Macmillan, 2011).

Hanman, Natalie, 'Kamila Shamsie: Where is the American writer writing about America in Pakistan? There is a deep lack of reckoning', *Guardian*, 11 April 2014. https://www.theguardian.com/culture/2014/apr/11/kamila-shamsie-america-pakistan-interview

'Haunting Heroines: Greek Plays and Transnational Novels', Society of Fellows and Heyman Center for the Humanities, 28 June 2018. https://sofheyman.org/media/videos/haunting-heroines-greek-plays-and-transnational-novels

Kramatschek, Claudia, 'Interview with Kamila Shamsie: A Dark Chapter in Pakistan's History', *Qantara*, 23 October 2009.

O'Keeffe, Alice, 'Kamila Shamsie in conversation about the changing nature of friendship in her latest novel, Best of Friends', *Bookseller*, 10 June 2022. https://www.thebookseller.com/author-interviews/kamila-shamsie-in-conversation-about-the-changing-nature-of-friendship-in-her-latest-novel-best-of-friends

'On Friendship, Politics and when the Two Collide, with Kamila Shamsie', *Shakespeare and Company* (podcast), 28 September 2022. https://shows.acast.com/sandco/episodes/on-friendship-politics-and-when-the-two-collide-with-kamila-

Rose, Jaya Battacharji, 'Interview: Kamila Shamsie on her Bold and Heart-Breaking New Novel, *Home Fire*'. https://www.jayabhattacharjirose.com/interview-kamila-shamsie-on-her-bold-and-heart-breaking-new-novel-home-fire/

Singh, Harleen, 'A Legacy of Violence: Interview with Kamila Shamsie about *Burnt Shadows*', *ARIEL*, 42:2 (2011), 157–162.

Thorpe, Vanessa, 'Kamila Shamsie: "Being a UK citizen makes me feel more able to take part in the conversation"', *Observer*, 27 August 2017.

Tolan, Fiona, '"I Don't Know Who I'd Be If I Wasn't a Writer": An interview with Kamila Shamsie', *Contemporary Women's Writing*, 13:2 (2019), 119–133.

Selected Scholarly Criticism

Ahmed, Rehana, 'Unsettling Cosmopolitans: Representations of London in Kamila Shamsie's *Salt and Saffron*', *Journal of Postcolonial Writing*, 40:1 (2002), 12–28.

———, 'Towards an ethics of reading Muslims: encountering difference in Kamila Shamsie's *Home Fire*', *Textual Practice*, 35:7 (2021), 1145–1161.

Banerjee, Debjani, 'From Cheap Labour to Overlooked Citizens: Looking for British Muslim Identities in Kamila Shamsie's *Home Fire*', *South Asian Review*, 41:3–4 (2020), 288–302.

Bowers, Maggie Ann, 'Asia's Europes: Anti-colonial attitudes in the novels of Ondaatje and Shamsie', *Journal of Postcolonial Writing*, 51:2 (2015), 184–195.

Chambers, Claire, 'Sound and Fury: Kamila Shamsie's *Home Fire*', *The Massachusetts Review*, 59:2 (2018), 202–219.

Cilano, Cara N., *National Identities in Pakistan: The 1971 War in Contemporary Pakistani Fiction* (London: Routledge, 2011).

———, *Contemporary Pakistani Fiction in English: Idea, Nation, State* (London and New York: Routledge, 2013).

Clements, Madeline, *Writing Islam from a South Asian Muslim Perspective: Rushdie, Hamid, Aslam, Shamsie* (Basingstoke: Palgrave Macmillan, 2016).

Gamal, Ahmed, 'The Global and the Postcolonial in Post-Migratory Literature', *Journal of Postcolonial Writing*, 49:5 (2012), 596–608.

Herbert, Caroline, 'Lyric Maps and the Legacies of 1971 in Kamila Shamsie's *Kartography*', *Journal of Postcolonial Writing*, 47:2 (2011), 159–172.

Kanwal, Aroosa, and Aslam, Saiyma (eds.), *Routledge Companion to Pakistani Anglophone Writing* (London and New York: Routledge, 2018).

Khan, Gohar Karim, 'Hideous Beauty of Bird-Shaped Burns: Transnational Allegory and Feminist Rhetoric in Kamila Shamsie's *Burnt Shadows*', *Pakistaniaat: A Journal of Pakistan Studies*, 3:2 (2011), 53–68.
King, Bruce, 'Kamila Shamsie's novels of history, exile and desire', *Journal of Postcolonial Writing*, 47:2 (2011), 147–158.
Lau, Lisa, and Mendes, Ana Cristina, 'Twenty-First Century Antigones: The Postcolonial Woman Shaped by 9/11 in Kamila Shamsie's *Home Fire*', *Studies in the Novel*, 53:1 (2021), 54–68.
Morey, Peter, *Islamophobia and the Novel* (New York: Columbia University Press, 2018).
Osman, Khan Touseef, 'The Struggle of Memory against Forgetting in Kamila Shamsie's *Salt and Saffron*', *Crossings: A Journal of English Studies*, 11:2 (2020), 133–148.
Ranasinha, Ruvani, 'Religion and Resistance in the Work of Kamila Shamsie', in Rehana Ahmed, Peter Morey, and Amina Yaqin (eds.), *Culture, Diaspora and Modernity in Muslim Writing* (New York and London: Routledge, 2012), 200–214.
Rutkowska, Urszula, 'The Political Novel in our still-evolving reality: Kamila Shamsie's *Home Fire* and the Shamima Begum case', *Textual Practice*, 36:6 (2022), 871–888.
Shirazi, Quratulain, 'Tradition and Modernity in Kamila Shamsie's *Salt and Saffron*', *International Journal of Language, Literature and Culture*, 1:2 (2014), 23–27.
Waterman, David, 'Karachi's Fragmented Interdependence: Kamila Shamsie's *In the City by the Sea*', *Alizés: Revue Angliciste de La Réunion*, Faculté des Lettres at Sciences Humains (Université de la Réunion, 2013), 194–206.
Weiss, Naomi, 'Tragic Form in Kamila Shamsie's *Home Fire*', *Classical Reception Journal*, 14:2 (2022), 240–263.
Windsor, Tara Talwar, 'Marginalized Memories and Multi-Layered Narratives of the Great War in Kamila Shamsie's *A God in Every Stone*', *Forum for Modern Language Studies*, 56:2 (2020), 229–246.
Yaqin, Amina, 'Necropolitical Trauma in Kamila Shamsie's Fiction', *The Muslim World*, III:2 (2021), 234–249.
Yaqoob, Munazza, and Hussain, Sofia, 'Changing Images of Pakistani Women in Kamila Shamsie's *Salt and Saffron* and *Broken Verses*', *Biannual Journal of Gender and Social Issues*, 11:2 (2012), 1–20.
Zinck, Pascal, 'Eyeless in Guantanamo: Vanishing Horizons in Kamila Shamsie's *Burnt Shadows*', *Commonwealth*, 33:1 (2010), 45–54.

Index

Adichie, Chimamanda Ngozi 12
Afghanistan 5, 6, 31, 39–43, 62, 69, 75
Ahmed, Rehana 20, 64, 78, 81
Al Qaeda 6, 43
 see also 9/11 terror attacks
Ali, Agha Shahid 3, 10, 77, 85n4
Annesley, James 80
anticolonialism 48, 50, 52, 53–54
archives 28–29
Ashby, Chloe 75
Aslam, Nadeem 94n14
 The Wasted Vigil 92n18

Banerjee, Debjani 60, 81
Bangladesh 2, 5, 26, 58, 79
Begum, Shamima 58, 81, 94n5
Benjamin, Walter 14
Berry, Lorraine 72
Bhutto, Benazir 7, 17–18
Bhutto, Zulfikar Ali 4, 6, 19, 26
Bowers, Maggie Ann 80, 92n13
burden of representation 8, 11, 82

Calvino, Italo 28
Chambers, Claire 40, 80
Cilano, Cara 28, 35, 45, 79, 90n18
citizenship 8, 12–13, 55–61, 66, 67, 74–76, 80–81, 94n5, 94n6
class
 inequality 21–23, 26–29, 71–73, 75–76
 limited literary representation 2, 11, 19, 78, 88n7

 wider literary representation 4, 56
Clements, Madeline 44, 80, 93n20
collage 29, 63–64, 81, 83
colonialism
 legacies 1, 4, 12, 13, 39–40, 57, 59–60, 82
 literary representation 47–54, 80
 mapping 29
corruption 4, 9, 15–19, 23, 68, 72–74, 86n16
cosmopolitanism 13, 20, 23, 78
 see also globalisation; transnational writing

Das, Santanu 80

English-language writing 10–11, 23
Eratosthenes 28

Faiz, Faiz Ahmed 33, 90n13, 90n14, 91n19
fantasy 15, 16–19, 78
 see also self-deception
Ferrante, Elena, *My Brilliant Friend* 70
Forster, E. M.
 Howards End 46, 54
 A Passage to India 46–47, 53
Foucault, Michel 73–74

Gamal, Ahmed 45, 80
geography 27–30, 47
 see also mapping

Ghalib, Mirza 10, 20
Gilroy, Paul 59
globalisation 46, 82
  see also cosmopolitanism; transnational writing
Guardian 8, 67, 94n6

Habibullah, Jahanara 2, 77
Hall, Stuart 28–29
Hameed, Yasmin 10
Hamid, Mohsin 77
  The Reluctant Fundamentalist 43
Hashmi, Ali Madeeh 33
Herbert, Caroline 25, 29, 79
history
  historical fiction 47–54, 80
  traces in the present 4, 6, 7, 25–26, 29–30, 59–60, 63, 77, 79, 82
  transnational literature 13–14, 16, 20–21, 40–47, 82–83
  see also time
homosexuality 35, 62, 68–69, 79
Hosain, Attia 2, 77
  Sunlight on a Broken Column 20
Hussain, Sofia 7, 78, 88n8

India
  history 2, 4–5, 20–21, 26, 32
  as literary setting 40–41, 46–54
  intertexts 12, 29, 30, 46–47, 53, 56, 63, 66, 70, 78, 81–82, 83
  Islamic State 56, 58, 61–63

Japan 39–42, 92n13
Javeri, Sabyn 11
Javid, Sajid 57–58, 93n3
Jay, Paul 12
Jinnah, Muhammad Ali 4
Johnson, Boris 67, 73, 95n24

Kadir, Djelal 94n14
Karachi
  history 8–9, 89n5
  as literary setting 3, 8, 9, 17, 18, 23, 25–29, 37, 64, 68–72
  Shamsie's residence in 2, 77
Kazi, Taha 32
Keeble, Arin 80
Khan, Ghaffar 48, 54
Khan, Gohar Karim 11
King, Bruce 4, 77
Kipling, Rudyard 43, 53

language 3, 4, 9–11, 22, 23, 36
Lau, Lisa 59, 81

mapping 27–29, 79, 89n5
  see also geography
martyrdom 37, 52, 65–66
May, Theresa 55, 57, 67
melancholia and mourning 36–37, 64–65
  imperial 59
Mendes, Ana Cristina 59, 81
migration
  chosen vs enforced 45, 79–80
  citizenship 8, 12–13, 55–61, 67, 72–75, 80–81, 94n5, 94n6
  discrimination 72–73, 75–76
  loss 77–78
  Mohajirs 9–10, 26–27, 45
Morey, Peter 46, 80, 95n14
mujahideen 6, 9, 31, 39, 42–43
multiple perspectives 29, 63–64, 81, 83
Musharraf, Pervaiz 7, 32
Muslims
  Britishness 57–60, 81
  Islamophobia 7–8, 44, 73, 95n24
  stereotypes 7, 59, 61, 64, 79, 81, 82
  treatment after 9/11 7–8, 13, 44, 56, 59–60, 64
mythic realism 12, 16–17, 47, 53, 57, 63–66, 78, 82

Naqvi, Tahir 32
national allegory 20, 24

nationalism 1, 4–5, 8–9, 26–27, 39–42, 46, 63
nationality *see* citizenship
9/11 terror attacks 6, 41–44
  treatment of Muslims after 7–8, 13, 44, 56, 59–60, 64
  see also 'War on Terror'

O'Gorman, Daniel 80
Ondaatje, Michael 3, 77
  The English Patient 46, 80, 92n13
Osman, Khan Touseef 22, 78

paired characters 22, 25, 26–27, 29–30, 52, 68–69
Pakistan
  ethnic nationalism 4, 8–10, 25–27
  history 2, 4–10, 26, 30–32, 49, 78–79
  Islamisation 7, 29, 30–31, 85n8
  migration to 2, 9, 26–27, 45
  1971 Civil War 2, 5, 26, 29, 79
  relations with United States 5–6, 31, 39–40, 42–43
  Shamsie's residence in 2, 67–68
  writers 11
  see also Karachi
Palestine 3, 90n14
Partition 2, 4, 9, 20–21, 26, 41, 79
poetry 3, 10, 33, 36, 79, 87n23, 90n13, 91n19
power
  abuses of 4, 9, 15–19, 23, 68, 72–74, 86n16
  imperial 50–51
  patriarchal 68–71, 78
  and powerlessness 15–19, 24, 66, 71–76
  and resistance 1, 18, 47, 78
Propp, Vladimir 52

Qissa Khwani massacre 52, 53–54

queer desire and sociality 35, 62, 68–69, 79
quests 16, 47, 52–53

Ranasinha, Ruvani 35, 79
Riaz, Fehmida 36, 91n19
Rushdie, Salman, *Midnight's Children* 24
Rutkowska, Urszula 66, 81, 94n5

Sayyid, Salman 92n16
Scott, Paul, *Raj Quartet* 53
securitisation after 9/11 6, 7–8, 13, 56, 59
self-deception 36, 62
  see also fantasy
Shah, Bina 11
Shaikh, Farzana 89n7, 91n20
Shakespeare, William 78
  A Midsummer Night's Dream 30
Shamsie, Kamila
  awards 3, 86n16
  Best of Friends 3, 7, 8, 9, 19, 35, 67–76, 96n3
  Broken Verses 3, 7, 10, 24, 30–37, 39, 52, 54, 79, 80
  Burnt Shadows 3, 6, 10, 19, 24, 39–47, 53, 79–80
  'Everest is Climbed' 55
  'Exiled' 94n6
  A God in Every Stone 47–54, 55, 80
  Home Fire 3, 7, 8, 19, 29, 30, 47, 52, 54, 55–66, 80–82
  In the City by the Sea 3, 7, 9, 15–19, 78
  journalism 8, 67
  Kartography 3, 5, 6, 9, 25–30, 34, 68, 78, 79, 80, 88n7
  life xi–xii, 2–3, 55, 77
  'Mulberry Absences' 77–78
  Offence: The Muslim Case 3, 31, 42, 85n8
  'Pop Idols' 95n21

Salt and Saffron 2, 7, 19–24, 52, 78–79
short stories 86n16
Shamsie, Muneeza 2
Shamsie, Saman 2
Shirazi, Quratulain 24
Siddiqa, Ayesha 86n11
Slovo, Gillian, *Another World: Losing Our Children to Islamic State* 62
Soja, Edward 28
Sontag, Susan 64
Sophocles, *Antigone* 12, 56, 63, 81, 94n13, 98n26
storytelling 16, 19–20, 23, 24, 49
Strabo 28
Syria 56, 58, 61–62, 80

television 32, 34–35, 69, 71
time
  multiple time signatures 25–26, 29, 48, 63
  pendular 18, 78
  see also history
Toor, Saadia 6
transnational writing 3–4, 11–14, 46, 55–56, 63, 77–80, 82–83
  see also cosmopolitanism; globalisation
Trapido, Barbara 88n7

United Kingdom
  Brexit 66–67
  immigration and citizenship 4, 8, 55–61, 67–68, 72–75, 80–81
  as literary setting 55–61, 67, 72–76
  patriarchal culture 50–51
  Shamsie's residence in 3, 8, 11, 55
United States
  foreign policy 5–6, 31, 32, 39–40, 42–45
  as literary setting 43–45

migration to 4, 27, 41, 44, 60
Shamsie's residence in 2–3
see also 9/11 terror attacks; 'War on Terror'; World War Two
Urdu
  language 9–10, 23, 36
  literature 10, 20, 36, 77, 79, 87n23, 90n13, 91n19

Veyret, Paul 82

Walkowitz, Rebecca 14
'War on Terror' 6, 8, 13, 30–32, 41–45, 60, 66
  see also 9/11 terror attacks; United States: foreign policy
Waterman, David 18, 78
Weiss, Naomi 81, 94n13
Windsor, Tara Talwar 54, 80
women
  martyrdom 37, 52, 65–66
  patriarchal societies 1, 7, 22, 30–31, 35, 40–41, 50–51, 62, 68–71, 78, 81
  political activism and resistance 7, 30–31, 34, 36, 52, 78
  stereotypes of Muslim 7, 61, 93n20, 95n24
  strong female characters 1, 7, 17–18, 34–35, 51, 52, 67, 78
wordplay 17, 23, 25, 36
World War One 48, 54, 80
World War Two 6, 39, 40, 42, 92n13

Yaqin, Amina 81, 87n23, 96n2
Yaqoob, Munazza 7, 78, 88n8
Young, Molly 74

Zia ul-Haq 6–7, 17, 19, 30–31, 36, 67, 71, 88n1, 89n7
Zinck, Pascal 80